YOUR
SPACEFLIGHT
MANUAL

YOUR SPACEFLIGHT MANUAL

HOW YOU COULD BE A TOURIST IN SPACE WITHIN TWENTY YEARS

DAVID ASHFORD AND PATRICK COLLINS

HEADLINE

First published in Great Britain in 1990
by HEADLINE BOOK PUBLISHING PLC
Headline House
79 Great Titchfield Street
London W1P 7FN

British Library Cataloguing in Publication Data

Ashford, David
    Your spaceflight manual.
    1. Space flight. Forecasts
    I. Title II. Collins, Patrick
    629.4'1

    ISBN 0-7472-0178-1

330

AN EDDISON SADD EDITION

Edited, designed and produced by
Eddison Sadd Editions Limited
St Chad's Court, 146B King's Cross Road
London WC1X 9DH

Phototypeset by Fingerprint Graphics Limited,
London
Origination by Columbia Offset, Singapore
Printed by Mandarin Offset in Hong Kong

These captions identify the vistas of space
from space printed in the preliminary pages
and on the endpapers of this book:

The image on the endpapers (inside the front and back
covers) shows the night sky seen from the southern
hemisphere. Forming a diamond shape at the centre of the
picture are the four bright stars known collectively as the
Southern Cross. The two bright stars on the right of the photograph are Alpha Centauri (to the right) and Beta Centauri (to
the left). Alpha Centauri is the third brightest star in the sky
and only 4.2 light years away from Earth; Beta Centauri, an
intensely-hot blue-white star, is 100 times further away.

The photograph on the first page (the half-title page) shows
jetstream clouds over Egypt and the Red Sea, as seen from
the Gemini 12 spacecraft. You can see the tip of the Sinai
Peninsula jutting into the Red Sea and the course of the River
Nile across the Egyptian Desert.

The photograph on page 3 (the title page) was taken from
Apollo 9 and shows a cloudy eddy off the west coast of
Morocco in North Africa. Spiralling clouds such as these are
formed whenever the wind is strong enough and there is
sufficient moisture in the air. The seaport in the top right-
hand corner is Agadir.

CONTENTS

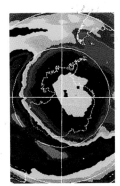

INTRODUCTION

Since the dawn of time people have looked up to the sky, the Moon, the Sun and the stars. What they saw or imagined there has been a vital and fascinating part of their quest for explanation and meaning. But only within the last two centuries have people been able to leave the Earth's surface, first in balloons, then in aeroplanes and, since 1961, in spacecraft.

There is a wide popular interest in space. Opinion polls suggest that about half the population would take a holiday in space if it were available at a price they could afford. On the other hand, far fewer people believe that they will visit space during their lifetime. The prohibitive cost of space travel, the dedication and training needed to become an astronaut, and the high risks involved have led to the general feeling that it will be many decades before space travel becomes safe enough, comfortable enough and, above all, cheap enough for holiday purposes. Present government plans for manned spaceflight (a large space station; a lunar base; and a visit to Mars) make no provision for the public to visit space.

Space tourism – the making of trips to orbit by fare-paying passengers – has received very little official attention. The consensus (to the extent that one can be said to exist) is that it should start around the middle of the next century. However, the idea is beginning to gain ground. A few companies and individuals have suggested that it could start much sooner and even that it should precede the large space station, the lunar base and the trip to Mars. The basic thinking was carried out in the early days of the Space Age, more than 20 years ago. Advances in engineering have now made the idea more practicable, yet space tourism is not even on the list of possible uses for the new American and European space stations.

What, then, would holidays in space be like and when are they likely to happen? This is the first book that tries to answer these questions. In the first four chapters we consider the feasibility of space tourism. Would it be popular? Why hasn't it been started before? What types of vehicle are needed? Can it be made safe? We

conclude that there is a very large demand for tourism to space; that if a space vehicle development pattern dictated by considerations of business and engineering rather than national defence and prestige had been followed, space tourism could be a reality now; and that there are no insurmountable safety problems. Furthermore, very little special technology would have to be developed; suitable vehicles could be built using, for example, engines already in production. If the development of space tourism takes place in the way we outline in this book, fares that are affordable by the rich could result in about ten years' time, and by people on middle incomes some seven years thereafter.

A trip in an aeroplane capable of flying into space and a stay in an orbiting hotel is the story told in Chapter 5. The highlights of the trip are the space-sports, such as flying and swimming, in low or zero gravity; and the breathtaking experience of seeing the Earth from space.

Chapter 6 draws the threads together and asks the inevitable question: what's the bottom line? We suggest that, by creating the large traffic levels needed to bring about airline-like travel to space at prices the public can afford space tourism holds the key to low-cost everyday space travel. The initial development costs could be surprisingly low. Part of the answer to the question we ask in this chapter is to consider the benefits of mass space travel to the human race: there are as many personal benefits as commercial ones. As we write, just over 200 chosen men and women have been in Earth orbit. All have said it was the experience of a lifetime.

Two chicken-and-egg situations stand in the way of space tourism. The first is that space tourism will require very low space transportation costs, but that high traffic levels are required to reduce costs, and these are achievable initially only with space tourism. The second is that government space agencies will not (on their past record) take space tourism seriously until asked to do so by the public or the travel business, but that the public and business women and men rely on government space agencies to tell them what opportunities in space are available. We hope this book will help break these two vicious circles.

The designing of space vehicles such as Spacecab (*see pages 42-49*) and Spacebus (*see pages 50-51*) is highly technical. Our aim, however, is that this book should be read not only by people who are familiar with the subject but by some of the future passengers of the space vehicles we describe. In order to make the text interesting to the non-technical, we have simplified it considerably. We therefore refer the technical reader requiring more rigorous analysis of our proposals and ideas to our technical papers listed under **Further Reading** on page 120.

Our feelings are that if this book encourages more ordinary people to think of travelling into space as something they might do in their lifetime, it will have served its purpose.

VISION OF THE FUTURE

Just as a holiday abroad changes the traveller's view of home, so will holidays in space change the way space tourists think of the Earth. Space tourism should encourage a world view, in which the Earth is seen as a frail spaceship on a long and hazardous journey. Observation from space holds one of the keys to scientific understanding of our impact on our environment and when millions of people per year visit space human concern for the well-being of the home planet will surely increase dramatically.

Many of today's problems require global action. Among them are the ever-present threat of nuclear war, mass poverty, mass starvation, pollution, dwindling wildlife and the using up of non-renewable resources. From space people will be able to watch these problems beginning, developing or worsening. Just as they now alarm the scientists who study them directly, so should they alarm space tourists who, one would think, would increase the pressure for political action.

From space national boundaries are invisible. So are the races, colours, tribes and creeds of the inhabitants they contain. The interdependence of the nations of the Earth is something

that can be seen from space. Long before the exploration of space began Tennyson appears to have had a similar vision, expressed in the poem *Locksley Hall* (1837/8). One critic, Philip Henderson, has interpreted it thus: '*Locksley Hall* contains much else besides Tennyson's youthful love affair. In it he turns hopefully to the world of action, to "the fairy tales of science", to visions of the future ...'

> For I dipt into the future, far as human eye could see,/Saw the Vision of the world, and all the wonder that would be;
>
> Saw the heavens fill with commerce, argosies of magic sails,/Pilots of the purple twilight, dropping down with costly bales;
>
> Heard the heavens fill with shouting, and there rained a ghastly dew/From the nations' airy navies grappling in the central blue;
>
> Far along the world-wide whisper of the south-wind rushing warm/With the standards of the peoples plunging through the thunder-storm;
>
> Till the war-drum throbbed no longer, and the battle-flags were furled/In the parliament of man, the Federation of the World.
>
> There the common sense of most shall hold a fretful realm in awe,/And the kindly earth shall slumber, lapt in universal law...
>
> ...Yet I doubt not through the ages one increasing purpose runs,/And the thoughts of men are widened in the process of the suns.

OVER TO YOU

Since democratic governments and business managers respond to public opinion, you can help to eliminate the chicken-and-egg situation outlined above by writing to airlines, travel companies and politicians to ask what they are doing about space tourism. If you want a space holiday, start asking (and saving) for it.

THE MARKET

1

If, back in 1904, someone had suggested to your great-grandfather that within a decade an airline service would be operating in America, he couldn't have been criticized for laughing. During 1904 the Wright Brothers made over 100 flights, but none stayed airborne for as long as five minutes. Most other experiments in flight had been heroic failures. The technology for journeys by air just didn't exist. Yet, sure enough, 1914 saw the world's first scheduled airline service: by flying boat across Florida, USA, from St Petersburg to Tampa.

Fast forward to the nineteen-nineties. Our suggestion that you might spend a holiday in space may surprise you, but it shouldn't make you laugh in disbelief. You've watched videos of astronauts walking on the Moon and orbiting in space stations. You've seen the Space Shuttle land on TV news. You know that the technology for getting people into space already exists. Your most likely response is going to be: 'When can I go?'.

If organizing trips into space depended on the technology alone our answer to this question would be simple: about ten years, the time it would take to build a passenger-carrying spacecraft. But a space project involves more than technology. Getting a spaceliner into scheduled operation depends as much on economic factors (is there a market for the product?) and political considerations (how would the government react?) as on the technical feasibility of the idea. All three factors, economic, political and technical, have to be set fair before funding is likely to be forthcoming. That's why it's going to take us a whole book to answer your simple question. And that's why, whenever the idea of space tourism is put to decision-makers in the space industry, they react in more or less the same way as your great-grandfather would probably have reacted to the idea of flying off for a summer holiday abroad, back in 1904.

DAY TRIPS INTO SPACE

It's amazing how the idea of passenger air services caught on. Just five years after the opening of that first flying boat service, the first international passenger airline was operating between London and Paris. Other services across the USA and Europe soon followed. You can imagine a similar response to the idea of space travel for the public. Since there are no colonies of people living out in space, ordinary people have no economic reason for wanting to get out there and back; but once someone starts the ball rolling by offering day trips into orbit, opinion polls suggest that within a few years the rich will be flying off to spend a week in a space hotel.

And it could all happen sooner than you think. Just as World War I was a catalyst for aircraft development, so World War II speeded the evolution of space rockets. But whereas air travel for popular and commercial purposes began directly after World War I, the exploration of space has remained in government hands, and space vehicles have been developed only for military or scientific purposes, or for reasons of national prestige. Moreover, the very high costs of spaceflight have deterred business people from investigating many of the commercial possibilities of space.

But the experience of manned spaceflight has shown it to be both attractive and potentially safe, and the few surveys that have been carried out suggest that people want to travel into space. In 1985 a Gallup survey of UK holiday habits for the American Express company recorded that out of a sample of 2,000 people interviewed, 63 per cent in the 16 to 24 age group would like to go to space. No costs were linked to the questions, but since in 30 years' time this group

A tour around a space station could become part of the itinerary of future space-trippers, since delivering essential supplies to space stations will become a useful and maybe even lucrative role for first-generation spaceliners. The earthbound tourists in the photograph (*left*) are exploring the mock-up of the first American space station, Skylab, in the Smithsonian Space Museum in Washington, USA. Skylab was launched in 1973 and used for research into space phenomena, but no successor has since been built. More space stations will be essential for research into astronomy, earth sciences and for the space engineering necessary for future space exploration.

will be in the over-45 age group – the population sector with the largest disposable income – these figures can be taken as indicative of a large total market for space tourism. We believe that passenger spacecraft could be built within ten years, using technology that exists already; and that the extension of the tourist industry into space could spearhead other commercial uses of space.

To see how all this might happen, we think it's worth taking a look at how air travel evolved, because we believe the space tourism industry will follow a broadly similar, four-phase development. The key question is: how many people will pay how much for trips to space at each of the phases?

THE PIONEERING PHASE

That first flying boat service heralded the beginning of the first of four broad phases in the development of air travel: the pioneering phase. This really began at the end of World War I as the obvious answer to a sudden surplus of war planes and air force pilots. For example, Pan Am started life in 1923 as a New York air taxi service, using nine ex-US navy flying boats salvaged from the scrapyard. European airlines such as Air France can trace their development back to scheduled air services run between European capitals, using converted warplanes. The passengers were pioneers as much as the crew: the flights were uncomfortable and not very reliable or safe, even by the standards of those times.

As in the pioneering phase of air travel, the sort of people who will want to be pioneer space tourists will be prepared to pay a very high price for a trip into orbit, perhaps as much as $1,000,000 (£600,000) for the earliest flights. Comfort and elaborate facilities will not be high on their list of priorities; they won't expect a prolonged stay in orbit and they will be prepared to stay in the spacecraft throughout the trip. Due to the high price of a ticket, the pioneering market may be expected to consist of a few very wealthy individuals or space enthusiasts: a few dozen per year at first, rising

to possibly 1,000 per year when the price has fallen to about $100,000 (£60,000).

For this initial phase quite a small spaceliner will be adequate: one with the capacity of a business jet, say six seats. Spacecab, our design for such a vehicle, is illustrated and explained on pages 42-43. The trip into space will be limited to a few orbits of the Earth, lasting for only about ten hours, just long enough to experience the fantastic views and the feeling of weightlessness.

THE GLAMOROUS, EXCLUSIVE PHASE

Although the passengers on the early airline flights were mostly wealthy, a progressive outlook distinguished them, more than a desire to travel in style. They probably dined out on their flying experiences for months afterwards. Air travel reached this exclusive phase only in the late nineteen-thirties. Converted warplanes had by this time been replaced by airliners, epitomized by the DC-3, which first flew in 1935 and is still in

Novelty and excitement are to be expected by passengers pioneering any new form of travel. Like these travellers clambering into the 1919 London-Paris Express, a De Havilland DH16 (*below*), tourists on the first spaceflights will have to be prepared to pay through the nose for what will probably be a muscle-cramping, stomach-lurching but wildly thrilling trip into the unknown. The bonuses: unlimited kudos and free dinner invitations for about a year.

service. This generation of airliners flew regular services between major European and American cities, and they were comfortable, safe and reliable.

What gives this phase of air travel development the label 'exclusive' is that the fares were well above anything ordinary people could afford. The passengers were, therefore, the well-off: business people; service and diplomatic personnel; and film stars bent on travelling with panache, who would pose for the cameras before boarding a flight from New York to Los Angeles. Since air travel was now considered safe enough even for politicians and royalty, the Prince of Wales, later (briefly) King Edward VIII, flew to his investiture; and the notorious photograph of the British Prime Minister, Neville Chamberlain, returning from his meeting with Hitler in Munich in 1938, with a piece of paper in his hand that was supposed to bring peace in our time, had in the background the Lockheed which had flown him there and back.

As space tourism goes into its second, 'exclusive', phase, more frequent services will become available. Prices will remain high by comparison with average expenditure on leisure pursuits, so customers will be primarily from high income groups, but also people in middle income groups who are prepared to save for a few years.

A larger vehicle, the size of a small airliner, will be needed for this phase. Spacebus, our design for a suitable vehicle, is described and illustrated in Chapter 3 (*see pages 50-51*) and in Chapter 5 (*see pages 72-73*). The trips will last longer – perhaps for two or three days and nights, so it will be necessary to build hotels out in space in which passengers can stay overnight.

Surveys suggest that around 1,000,000 people per year would each pay $10,000 (£6,000) for a short stay in space. This may seem large by comparison with present manned spaceflight levels: just 200 astronauts have been into space since the first manned flight in 1961. However, this number is tiny compared with present commercial air transport levels of around 1,000,000,000 passengers per year.

SPACE TOURISM REACHES MATURITY

By the mid-nineteen-sixties the use of jet airliners had become widespread. Speed, comfort, safety and reliability were all much improved and fares were within reach of most people. This was the mature phase of air travel. Jets could cross the Atlantic, and more people were flying over than sailing across it. Package tours based on air travel had become big business.

When space travel reaches the mature phase costs will have fallen (through economies of scale, the benefits of experience and advances in engineering) far enough to bring the service within reach of a large proportion of the population. Many facilities will be available, both on board the spacecraft and in the large, elaborate hotels out in space, into which passengers will disembark to spend a few days orbiting the Earth. Turnover will be much higher than in the preceding phases. There will be competition between suppliers of services, leading to a continuing decline in prices and a corresponding growth in the total market.

A new generation of spaceliners will be required for this phase, using jet engines designed to operate up to very high speeds. They will be larger and more economical to run than Spacecab and Spacebus, but will not be radically different.

MASS MARKET SPACE TRAVEL

Within a decade air travel reached a new stage as the widebody jets – the Boeing 747 and the Airbus A300, for example – ushered in the mass phase of development. By the mid-nineteen-seventies air travel had become the standard means of middle- and long-distance passenger transport for business purposes. The route network had expanded to encompass almost every country in the world and standards of passenger comfort and safety were much higher than those of their predecessors. Today the aeroplane is taken for granted; the main problems facing the air traveller in the mass market phase are strikes, terrorism, delays due to congested airspace, baggage-handling mistakes, drunken passengers, sloppy service, and long queues for the car parks and the check-in desks. Air travel has come of age, it seems.

When space tourism has evolved to the mass phase it will be available to most of the population, at least at some stage in their lives. Although this, the ultimate evolution of space tourism, is clearly far in the future, it is nevertheless possible to envisage an industry on a scale approaching that of present-day air travel to tourist centres, with tens of millions of passenger flights per year to a variety of destinations in orbit.

It is too early to say what type of spacecraft will be developed for this phase. It may well be more like a spaceship from science fiction and not at all like an aeroplane. Space hotels will come in all shapes and sizes, and will have begun to develop distinct ambiances and to specialize in the facilities they offer. One might try to attract scientific and educational parties, for example, by installing advanced astronomy equipment; another might develop extensive space-sports facilities; and another might offer experimental dance and theatre. The better-off, by now experienced space traveller will now be heading for more expensive destinations on the Moon and perhaps even to the nearer planets in the Solar System.

By analogy with the development of **air travel** *(right)*, **a space tourism industry** will probably evolve in four broad stages *(top)*: a pioneering phase; an exclusive – glamorous – phase; a mature phase and a mass-market phase. But while air travel has taken all of the twentieth century to evolve, space travel might realistically begin to develop in as few as ten years from now. So, if the pioneering phase starts around the year AD2000, the mature phase, using a new generation of spaceliners, could be reached as early as the twenty-twenties. But this will happen only if the possibility of space tourism is taken seriously **now** by key people in the government.

Phase 1: Pioneering. Price per trip: about $1,000,000 (£600,000) falling to $100,000 (£60,000). Transportation: Spacecab. Duration of trip: say, ten hours. Projected timescale: starting around AD2000.

Phase 2: Exclusive. Price per trip: below $100,000 (£60,000) falling to $10,000 (£6,000). Transportation: Spacebus. Duration of trip: ten hours to a few days, possibly including a stopover at a space station. Projected timescale: starting around AD2005.

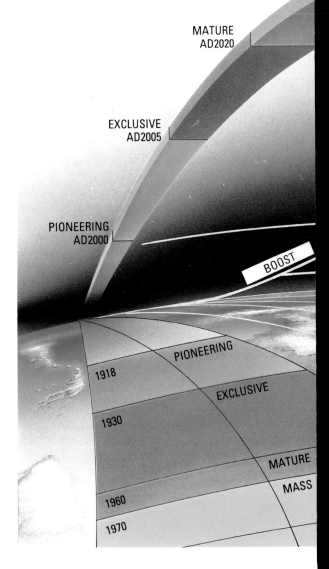

MATURE
AD2020

EXCLUSIVE
AD2005

PIONEERING
AD2000

BOOST

PIONEERING

1918

EXCLUSIVE

1930

MATURE

MASS

1960

1970

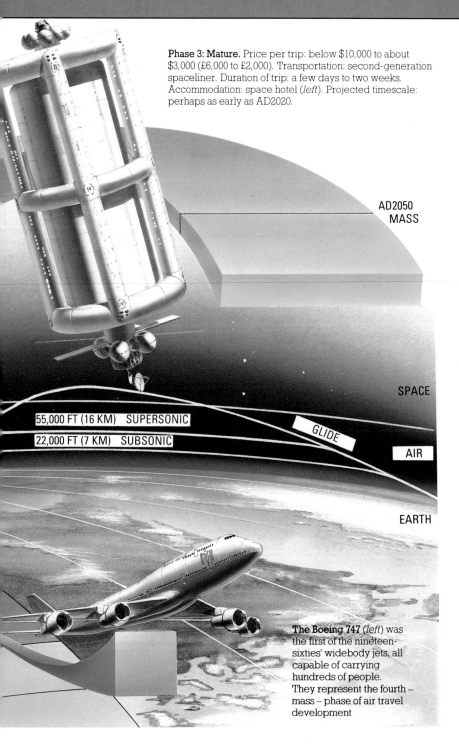

Phase 3: Mature. Price per trip: below $10,000 to about $3,000 (£6,000 to £2,000). Transportation: second-generation spaceliner. Duration of trip: a few days to two weeks. Accommodation: space hotel (*left*). Projected timescale: perhaps as early as AD2020.

AD2050
MASS

55,000 FT (16 KM) SUPERSONIC

22,000 FT (7 KM) SUBSONIC

GLIDE

SPACE

AIR

EARTH

The Boeing 747 (*left*) was the first of the nineteen-sixties' widebody jets, all capable of carrying hundreds of people. They represent the fourth – mass – phase of air travel development

Phase 4: Mass. Price per trip: less than $3,000 (£2,000). Transportation: third-generation (advanced) spaceliner. Duration of trip: say, one to two weeks. Accommodation: large space hotel. Projected timescale: perhaps around the year AD2050.

Sub-orbital transport. A likely development during phase 3, the mature phase of space travel evolution. Price per trip: about $5,000 (£3,000). Transportation: sub-orbital airliner (also called a boost-glider), derived from second-generation spaceliners. Duration of trip: just over an hour Delhi to New York (about one and a half hours to encircle the Earth).

The intercontinental airliner of the future could be a sub-orbital airliner, a semi-spacecraft which flies much higher and faster than a fourth-generation airliner spending part of each flight effectively out in space. After take-off, rocket engines will boost the craft to 90% of the speed at which a satellite travels, and to a height of over 100 mls (160 km). It will then glide back into the atmosphere, to land half-way round the world from its launch site just over an hour later.

SUB-ORBITAL AIRLINERS

Space tourism aside, developing a spaceliner would be a worthwhile project for other commercial reasons. One of the twentieth century's obsessions – the urge to cut down the time it takes to cross the globe from A to B – is unlikely to end with Concorde or, indeed, with the second millennium. Sub-orbital aircraft (also called boost-glide planes) have been under study for many years. Indeed, during World War II the Germans had a project for an 'antipodal bomber' which would have taken off from Germany, accelerated to just short of the speed required to achieve orbit, bombed New York and landed in Japan. This project was clearly not practicable with the materials then available, but it had a significant influence on post-World War II thinking in Europe, the USA and the USSR.

The principle on which sub-orbital craft work is simple: if the rocket motors of a spaceliner were shut down just before it reached orbit it would immediately start to descend on a long glide path. A speed of 90 per cent of satellite speed would give it enough range to land halfway round the world from its take-off point. The flight time would be about 75 minutes.

Research shows that many passengers would be prepared to pay a premium fare for such a high-speed service, though probably no more than $5,000 (£3,000). Sub-orbital airliner services are likely to become available as an offshoot of passenger spacecraft development, but probably not until the mature phase. The early spaceliners will be able to attract significant numbers of people at much higher prices during the earliest phases of space tourism, but sub-orbital airliners will have to compete in the market place with subsonic airline services; in order to operate economically at lower prices they will have to be more advanced technically than the early spaceliners.

SPACE STATIONS

Research laboratories orbiting the Earth could be useful for several reasons. If they were big enough for teams of scientists to live and work in for a few months at a time, they could be used for research in the fields of astronomy, earth sciences and space engineering. Studies could be carried out on the effects of zero gravity on animals, plants and physical processes: on the mixing and solidification of liquids; on the growth of crystals and on chemical reactions. Once launched into space, these laboratories – or space stations – would stay in orbit for years on end, needing only regular visits by supply vehicles to change crews, top up consumables, bring up urgent spare parts and return the results of the experiments.

Space stations are not a new idea. The first, the American Skylab, was launched in 1973, but as we write the Russian Mir station (*see page 52*) is the only one in orbit. The high cost of the supply flights is the main reason for this lack of progress: space stations are still very expensive to maintain.

There are plans to assemble a large NASA/ International space station, using the Space Shuttle for supply missions, but at a cost of $300,000,000 (£180,000,000) per Space Shuttle flight, very few visits would be possible and this would heavily restrict its use. Even a factor of only ten less than the Space Shuttle – about $400,000 (£300,000) per seat – would be a major improvement. According to our calculations this would be attainable using Spacecab during the pioneering first phase of space tourism development. Later spaceliners offer the promise of much lower costs, which will considerably reduce the expense of supplying a space station and thus greatly increase the frequency of visits possible.

This crucial reduction in costs would make the development of space stations for commercial uses financially feasible. They could be used as factories for the manufacture of certain products under zero gravity; for collecting solar power and beaming it to Earth (this will require solar panels several miles across); and as staging posts for journeys to more distant places in space for exploration, mining rare materials in other heavenly bodies and eventually for col-

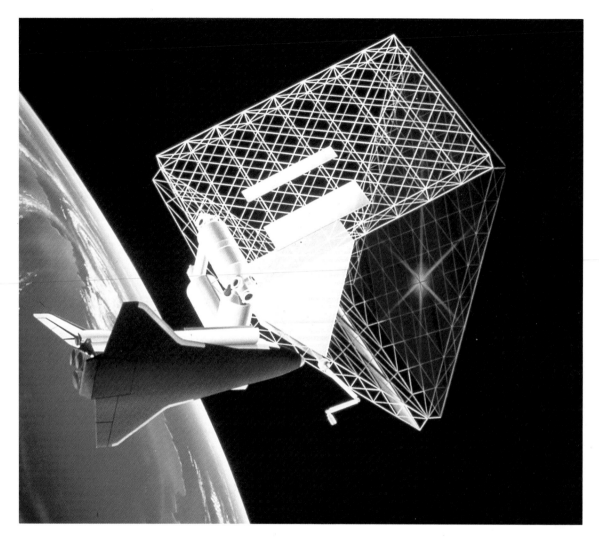

onization. The demand curve on page 17 gives preliminary estimates of how such activities will increase as costs are reduced.

BACK TO THE PRESENT

In all the potential uses of spaceliners discussed so far, the person or company using the service would be paying for the regular transportation of weighty items, such as people, spare parts and other supplies, and high-value cargo. Because of

The NASA Freedom Space Station (*early concept above*) will be an orbiting laboratory in which up to eight astronauts will carry out scientific research. It is to be launched during the nineteen-nineties, so the design is evolving as we write, but this artist's impression shows it to be large and rather elaborate. It is very expensive with a total cost of $20 billion, (£12.5 million). The Space Shuttle will have to make special trips into space to launch and to service it. The high cost of using the Shuttle to provide these essential services will greatly restrict its use, however. Passenger-carrying spacecraft making trips into space could service space stations as part of their scheduled operations, thus reducing the costs, eventually, to less than 1% of the Shuttle's costs.

15

the current high costs of launching such items, today's commercial uses of space have been restricted to those in which the end product is the transmission of large quantities of information in the form of a stream of virtually weightless electronic data down a radio link.

Commercial satellites, for example, use the unique perspective of the Earth from space for receiving and transmitting large quantities of data for communications, meteorology, Earth-viewing and navigation. In each case a satellite receives data (radio or TV transmissions, video data on cloud formations or aspects of the Earth's surface); processes it; and transmits it back to the receiving station on Earth. These satellites are now so reliable that they can operate with no maintenance at all for several years. During this operational period they can handle so much data that a profit can be made in spite of the enormous cost of launching them.

Ariane (*see page 44*) is designed to launch communications satellites. The latest version, Ariane 4, can launch two satellites at a high cost of some $30,000,000 (£18,000,000) each. The Space Shuttle can launch satellites at broadly similar costs. Some 200 tonnes of commercial satellites are currently being launched each year at a cost of around $10,000,000 (£6,000,000) per tonne. These enormous costs have held back further exploitation of space.

Spaceliners designed for passenger-carrying would have a hold too small for the largest communications satellites. However, they could carry smaller satellites to be launched in space and could ferry specialist mechanics to assemble and repair very large satellites in orbit.

BUILDING A SPACELINER FLEET

The breakthrough in transportation of both passengers and cargo into space will occur during the exclusive phase of the development of space tourism. This will be a major turning point for the space industry and it is therefore an important milestone to aim for. Developments thereafter will follow their own course, led by what the market wants.

Until such routine public transport is available, the space industry will be limited to expensive, government-funded projects for prestige, defence or scientific research; and to the few applications for unmanned satellites for which a commercial market exists, such as communications. The DC-3 of the space age will, therefore, be a spaceliner capable of making a profit for its operator at a fare level of about $10,000 (£6,000), at a traffic level of about 1,000,000 passengers per year. This would require a fleet of about 50 spaceliners.

WHEN CAN YOU GO?

Given a fair wind – assuming, that is, that the development of space tourism becomes a major international objective in the nineteen-nineties – you could expect to be able to take a trip into space during the first decade of the twenty-first century. We suggest that a prototype of a small spaceliner, Spacecab (see pages 42-43), could be flying within seven years. It could be used for carrying professional astronauts to and from space stations. Within three more years it could have a Certificate of Airworthiness and could be used for carrying passengers on trips into space, consisting of a few orbits of the Earth. A more advanced passenger vehicle, Spacebus (*see pages 50-51*) could follow two years later with a fare of some $100,000 (£60,000), marking the beginning of the exclusive phase of development. About 5 years later (17 years from now), a more advanced version of Spacebus could be operating at prices of $10,000 (£6,000). The launching of hotels in space will follow a few years behind spaceliners.

These timescales are far shorter than the view that is currently accepted. Progress can be so rapid because it is possible to build on technical developments that have already been made, as the next two chapters will show. The technical requirements and a realistic timescale within which they could be achieved are detailed in Chapter 3. Economic considerations – the bottom line – are discussed in Chapter 6.

Unfortunately, however, we cannot make a

guess at the starting date, since before any program of space travel can be put into operation the biggest problem of all must be overcome. That is: how to get the government and those important decision-makers in the aerospace and travel industries to accept that a large market for space travel exists; that space tourism, and not projects set up for military strategy or national prestige, can ensure the high traffic levels and revenues to make investing in the commercial development of spaceliners a worthwhile enterprise.

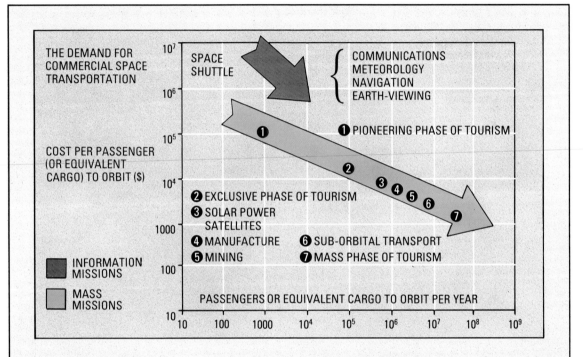

THE DEMAND FOR COMMERCIAL SPACE TRANSPORTATION

COST PER PASSENGER (OR EQUIVALENT CARGO) TO ORBIT ($)

SPACE SHUTTLE

COMMUNICATIONS METEOROLOGY NAVIGATION EARTH-VIEWING

❶ PIONEERING PHASE OF TOURISM

❷ EXCLUSIVE PHASE OF TOURISM
❸ SOLAR POWER SATELLITES
❹ MANUFACTURE
❺ MINING
❻ SUB-ORBITAL TRANSPORT
❼ MASS PHASE OF TOURISM

INFORMATION MISSIONS

MASS MISSIONS

PASSENGERS OR EQUIVALENT CARGO TO ORBIT PER YEAR

The arrow in the graph shows that as the cost per seat or equivalent freight on a spaceliner is reduced, new uses of space will become possible. Though the numbers used are merely informed guesses, the tentative demand curve they produce amounts to a clear pattern of the development of space transportation. Uses of space at today's very high costs are limited to specialized commercial information missions, of which communications is the most important, and to government-funded defence, prestige and scientific uses. The likely commercial uses of spaceliners are arranged in the graph in descending order of their possible costs – and, therefore, the order in which they will become commercially viable – from supplying space stations to pioneering and developing the use of space as a tourist venue, to industrial and other uses. Thus, space tourism should be the first use to justify the development of spaceliners, and it should therefore be the driving force behind lower space transportation cost.

THE BACKGROUND

2

If spaceliners can be built using existing technology; if their development would make possible passenger flights and thus the extension of tourism into space; and if they would facilitate other commercial uses of space, why have they not yet been developed? And why is the tourism potential of space so rarely mentioned by government agencies or in the technical press? The answers to these questions lie in the complex network of historical and political factors which have determined the evolution of Western rockets and other spacecraft, especially during the second half of the twentieth century.

A LONG LOOK BACK

Rocket fireworks have been used for many hundreds of years and may have been used in ancient times to celebrate religious festivals, but the idea of exploiting rockets for other peaceful purposes is almost new. Perhaps because war is so obvious an application for an object that can fly fast through the air, trailing spectacular tails of flame, and make a thunderous noise on impact, rockets have been used in war throughout their 1,000-year-long history. Despite the inaccuracy of the first artillery rockets, they were deployed by warring generals from at least the beginning of the second millennium in China, in the Middle East and in Europe. Between the tenth century (in China, where they were called 'flame arrows') and the nineteenth century (in England, where a Colonel William Congreve refined crude pyrotechnic devices into effective artillery rockets), the accuracy, force of impact and range of rockets were gradually improved until,

The X-15 suspended from beneath a B-52 bomber in this photograph (*left*), from where it was launched, represents the acme of the development of high-speed, rocket-powered aircraft, which began in the nineteen-twenties with the application of a rocket engine to a sailplane. Since it was air-launched, the X-15 could be made heavier than if it had had to take off under its own power, so it could carry more fuel and so fly higher and faster. The evolution of rocket-powered aircraft culminated in 1968 with the last flight of the X-15, the most successful high-speed research aeroplane, but the last rocket-powered aeroplane to be built.

by the middle of the nineteenth century rocket missiles had become effective army equipment.

But in times of peace rockets, along with many other wartime inventions, have been adapted to pacific uses. In the early nineteenth century, for example, they were put to work carrying lifelines to storm-endangered ships. Around the turn of the century came a still more spectacular peaceful application: the invention of the first rocket-powered space vehicle by a Russian physicist, Konstantin Tsiolkovsky. He realized that rocket motors, unlike any other known type of engine, would work in space; and, with amazing foresight, he specified as its propellants liquid oxygen and liquid hydrogen, which are used by today's high-performance rockets. Then, in 1926, the first liquid-propellant rocket was successfully launched; its designer was an American, Robert Goddard.

As a result of the achievements of a coterie of German rocket engineers, who had begun experimenting with rockets after the Versailles Treaty of 1919 imposed restrictions on flying aircraft, rockets began to enter the mainstream of history during the nineteen-thirties. The celebrated space engineer, Wernher von Braun, and his contemporaries made a number of important technological advances in space rocketry. When war broke out von Braun was detailed to produce rocket-propelled missiles for the military. His advances led to the development of ICBMs (Intercontinental Ballistic Missiles), to the space race and to the first person on the Moon.

It was recognized by these pioneers of space travel that there are two ways of getting a spacecraft into orbit. You can blast it off vertically – the ballistic approach, used by Tsiolkovsky and Goddard; or you can design a winged vehicle and fly it into orbit – the aeroplane approach.

The word 'ballistic', as in 'ballistic missile' or 'ballistic re-entry', means that the vehicle so described has no wings; and that aerodynamic lift is relatively unimportant to the way it moves through the air. The craft flies in more or less the same way that a ball or a large stone does if you throw it upwards. In short, the difference between ballistic flight and winged flight is essentially the difference between the way a ball and a paper dart behave in the air.

A ballistic vehicle takes off vertically, upheld by the thrust of its motors; and climbs into near space before turning over into a more or less horizontal position to accelerate to the high speeds required to escape into orbit. The atmosphere hinders the ascent by imposing a drag force on the craft. Rocket motors are the natural choice for this type of vehicle because they give very high thrust for a given weight; and because the portion of the ascent that passes through the Earth's atmosphere is too short to justify the use of air-breathing (jet) engines, which use less fuel but are heavier. Wings can be added to ballistic vehicles so that they can fly to an airfield after re-entering the Earth's atmosphere, but they are not required for the ascent to orbit.

An alternative design is a spaceplane. This is an aeroplane in all engineering essentials: it takes off horizontally and uses its wings to provide supporting lift. It accelerates to the speed which will take it into orbit on a gentle climb path. Air-breathing (jet) engines are the natural choice for take-off and the early part of the ascent through the lower atmosphere; and rocket engines to take over at speeds too high for the jets to work.

ROCKETING INTO SPACE

The first vehicles capable of accelerating close to the speeds needed to pass through the upper atmosphere into orbit were rocket-powered ballistic missiles driven by the needs of war: first hot; then Cold. The first large rocket-powered vehicle, and the first ballistic missile, was the V-2, which was designed and manufactured by the Germans during World War II and used against the British during the last year of the war. Its design formed the model for the post-war American and Soviet intercontinental ballistic missiles developed during the Cold War (see page 23). Fitted with nuclear warheads and capable of flying one-third of the way around the Earth in about half an hour, they are still the most devastating weapons the world has ever seen and the hardest to defend against.

It was natural, therefore, that the first peaceful application of the rocket technology that had been developed during World War II and the Cold War – the space exploration missions of the nineteen-fifties and nineteen-sixties – should have used converted ballistic missiles. These devices were being built at the time, and, unlike winged designs they needed no pilots or cockpits, wings, tails, heat-shields or landing-gear, so they were lighter and easier to send into orbit.

FLYING INTO ORBIT

Among the most memorable of the peacetime developments in rocket technology was the design for the first rocket-powered aircraft. It is especially memorable because it was conceived while in prison awaiting execution by Nikolai Kibalchich, one of the Russian designers of the bomb that killed Czar Alexander II. A rocket-powered aircraft – a converted Ente sailplane – first flew in Germany in 1928. Later that year car manufacturer Fritz von Opel achieved 95 miles per hour (about 153 kilometres per hour) in a glider propelled by Sander solid-propellant rockets; and 125 miles per hour (about 200 kilometres per hour) in a rocket-powered Rak racing car. In 1935 the Germans fitted a rocket engine to a high-performance fighter plane, the Heinkel He 112.

The general aim of the German and Austrian rocket designers of the time seems to have been to fly progressively faster and higher until orbit was reached. This idea was pioneered by Professor Eugene Sänger, a Viennese engineer who is generally credited as having been the first to investigate the principles of high-speed rocket-powered sub-orbital or orbital aeroplanes. Raketenflugtechnik, a book written by Sänger in 1933, contains a design for a high-speed research aircraft, looking remarkably like the American X-15 designed 25 years later (*see page 25*). Early in World War II he progressed to the design of a sub-orbital bomber, intended to take off using a rocket-powered sled on tracks. After take-off its own rocket engines would accelerate the bomber to 80 per cent of satellite speed at a height of over 100 miles (160 kilometres), effectively out in space. It would then re-enter the atmosphere and land half way round the world from the launch site. On the way it would drop a bomb. This project was never built; the military expressed interest in it, but Sänger's design was too far ahead of its time. Nevertheless it inspired much of the post-World War II work on winged and rocket vehicles carried out in Europe and in the USA.

The first rocket aeroplane to enter service was the Messerschmitt Me 163. It was used as a fighter towards the end of World War II and achieved limited success against the Allied bombing raids. It was by far the fastest aero-

continued on page 24

THE LANGUAGE OF SPACE TRAVEL

For the benefit of readers who are unfamiliar with aerospace terminology, it is useful at this point to explain a few key terms and concepts. A **spacecraft** is a vehicle that travels in space: communications satellites; the Space Shuttle Orbiter; Skylab and space hotels are all spacecraft. Early spacecraft had no rocket motors (many still do not) and they had to be transported through the Earth's atmosphere and launched into orbit by a **launch vehicle** (sometimes called a **launcher**). This, then, may be defined as a craft designed to take off from Earth and to carry a spacecraft, such as a satellite, into space and place it in orbit. All launch vehicles built so far have blasted off vertically.

The upper stages of some launch vehicles (such as the Lockheed Agena and the Space Shuttle Orbiter) have been designed to do useful jobs in orbit, other than launching satellites, and some satellites have been fitted with built-in rocket motors. Thus the distinction between launch vehicles and spacecraft is tending to become blurred.

It has not yet been possible to build a launch vehicle which can fly into orbit as just one vehicle. Engineers have had to design launchers as a series of vehicles, stacked one on top of another. Each separate vehicle in the stack is called a **stage.** The lower stage is called a **booster.** After the booster has used up its fuel, the engines of the second stage are started and the booster separates away from the upper stages and falls or flies back to Earth. The second stage increases speed and travels on until it achieves orbit, or until its fuel supply is exhausted; then the third stage takes over, and so on. By the last, upper, stage the vehicle has accelerated to the velocity required to reach orbit. Two or three stages are usual.

A logical development of the booster stage, the **flyback booster,** is a vertical take-off ballistic booster fitted with wings so it can be flown back to base. The upper stage may, like the upper stage of the Space Shuttle, be manned and designed to operate in orbit, and is called an **orbiter.**

A **spaceplane** has wings and can take off horizontally and fly into space. A spaceplane may be a launch vehicle, designed to carry spacecraft into orbit; or it can be, like Spacebus, a combined launch vehicle/spacecraft. Spacebus's lower stage, called the booster, provides the thrust to propel the craft through the atmosphere; and its upper stage is called an orbiter because it carries a crew and is designed to operate in orbit. No spaceplane has yet been built. A **spaceliner** is our term for a spaceplane designed to carry passengers.

EVOLUTION OF US LAUNCH VEHICLES

PHASE 1: BALLISTIC MISSILES

1943: The German V-2 rocket (1) was the first vehicle capable of reaching space and also the first large rocket-powered vehicle. It was kept up initially by the thrust of the rocket motor and, after burn-out (when all the fuel was used up) it simply followed the trajectory on which it had been set, using neither power nor aerodynamic lift. Subsequent post-World War II American and Soviet ballistic missiles and the first space launch vehicles were all derived from the V-2.

1953: The Redstone ballistic missile (2) was the first major new product the German-born rocket engineers developed for the US Army after 1945. In effect it was an enlarged V-2. It formed the lower stage of the **Juno launcher (3)** , which put the first American satellite into orbit in 1958, in rapid response to the launching of the Soviet Sputnik 1 in 1957. The Redstone was also used as the booster for the **Redstone-Mercury (4)**, which made the first American manned sub-orbital spaceflight in May 1961, shortly after Yuri Gagarin became the first man in space in the Vostok 1 spacecraft in April 1961. On this flight Commander Alan Shepard, USN, reached a height of 116 mls (187 km) before landing in the Atlantic in his Mercury capsule.

PHASE 2: SPIN-OFFS

The launch vehicles derived from the **Thor IRBM** (Intermediate-Range Ballistic Missile) **(5)**, such as the **Thor-Agena (6)** and the **Delta II (7)**, started a second phase of development. Thor was declared operational in 1959 and in the early nineteen-sixties was deployed in the UK by the USAF and the RAF. The most used has been the Thor-Delta (the launcher is now called Delta). In 1960 Atlas was the first American ICBM to enter service. In 1962 it was used to launch Lt-Col (now Senator) John Glenn, the first US astronaut, into orbit in his Mercury space capsule; his flight lasted just under five hours. Various upper stages of Atlas and Thor have been used in their launcher derivates, and in 1962 Centaur was the

first to use liquid hydrogen fuel. The Atlas-Centaur is still in production. The Titan ICBM followed Atlas into service in 1962. Its latest launcher version, Titan 4, can launch 15 tonnes into low orbit.

PHASE 3: SATURN LAUNCHERS

The Apollo lunar programe in the sixties necessitated the development of the **Saturn 1B (8)** and the **Saturn V (9)**. These, the largest Western launch vehicles yet built, carried out 22 launches without a failure between 1961 and the final launch, for the Apollo-Soyuz mission of 1975. The Saturn 1B was designed to test the technology for Saturn V, in particular engines clustered together. Saturn V, the heaviest flying machine yet produced, was the definitive vehicle for the Moon programme. It had an overall length of 364 ft (111 m) and a lift-off weight of 2,700 tonnes. It could launch over 100 tonnes to low orbit – three times the payload of the Shuttle. On a cost per tonne basis it cost less than the Shuttle, although no part of it was reusable.

PHASE 4: SPACE SHUTTLE

This phase began around the early nineteen-seventies with the start of the Space Shuttle development programme; the first orbital flight took place in 1981. The **Space Shuttle (10)** has three major components: the Orbiter, a delta-winged aeroplane which carries a flight crew of two and up to eight astronauts; and a payload of up to 30 tonnes in a large cargo bay 15 ft (4.5 m) in diameter and 60 ft (18 m) long. It can stay in orbit for up to ten days. Its three powerful motors use propellant from the large External Tank. This is discarded just short of orbit, then re-enters the atmosphere and either burns up or lands in the ocean. The early part of the ascent is assisted by two Solid Rocket Boosters, which descend by parachute into the sea after burn-out; are recovered, stripped down and cleaned, and selected components are refurbished and put back on to the assembly line. At lift-off the Shuttle weighs some 2,000 tonnes.

The American space programme gained impetus after World War II, with the transfer to the USA of V-2 rockets captured from the German army, together with leading members of their development team. The most famous of these German-born aerospace engineers was Wernher von Braun, who pioneered the V-2 rocket in the nineteen-forties. American space vehicles evolved in four major phases, illustrated here. European and Japanese developments have followed a similar pattern, but they began several years later and the scale of their development has been much smaller.

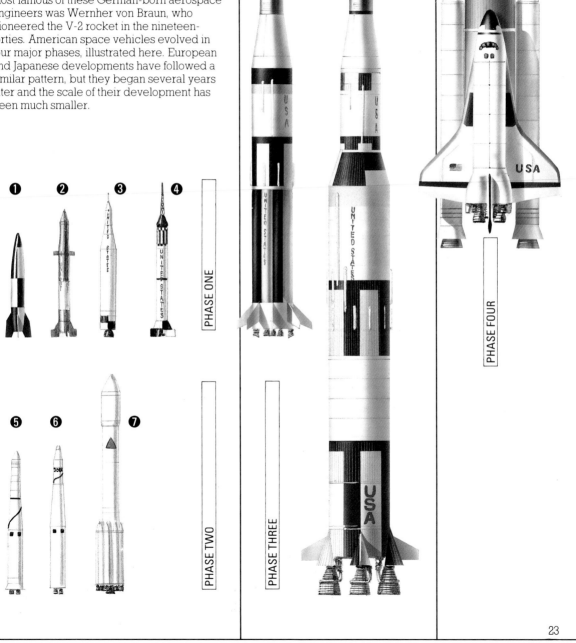

PHASE ONE

PHASE TWO

PHASE THREE

PHASE FOUR

plane in service during World War II but, fortunately for the Allies, it did not achieve technical maturity; numerous explosions of the rocket system made it very dangerous to fly. As an incidental curiosity, it was the last front-line fighter aircraft to have wings made of wood.

Towards the end of the war, two V-2s were fitted with wings, intended to increase their range. Thus, the winged V-2 (see opposite, 1) became the first large winged supersonic flying machine. The wings enabled the vehicle to glide to its target following re-entry into the Earth's atmosphere. The two examples were flown experimentally in 1945. The first exploded shortly after launch for reasons unconnected with the wings. The second accelerated to Mach 4 in a stable and controlled fashion and the experiment was declared a success (though the wings came off during re-entry). It was not until 16 years later, when the American X-15 reached Mach 4 for the first time (see below), that any winged vehicle flew faster.

A design was prepared for a piloted version of the V-2, with a pressurized cockpit in place of the warhead, and with flaps and landing-gear so that it could be brought down at an aerodrome. This vehicle was estimated to be capable of carrying a pilot 400 miles (about 644 kilometres) in 17 minutes, but it was never built.

The first manned device to exceed the speed of sound was a rocket-powered research aeroplane, the Bell X-1 (see opposite, 2), which accomplished this feat in 1947. It was followed by the Douglas Skyrocket, which was the first aeroplane to reach Mach 2 and the Bell X-2 (see opposite, 4), which was the first to reach Mach 3.

Perhaps the first practical rocket aeroplane, the SR.53 (see opposite, 3), was the prototype of a high-performance rocket-plus-jet interceptor fighter. It is the only British manned aeroplane designed from the outset with rocket motors to have flown. Two prototypes were built and an operational version was cancelled in 1957.

Generally recognized to have been the most successful high-speed research aeroplane of all time, the North American X-15 (see opposite, 5) first flew in 1959. Its top speed was one quarter of satellite speed and it could zoom-climb briefly into space. It proved much of the technology needed for the Apollo programme and later for the Space Shuttle.

And there the 40-year sequence of ever-faster rocket aeroplanes came to an end. Had development continued a spaceplane could have been built in the mid-nineteen-seventies, but today's launch vehicles (the vehicles which carry satellites and interplanetary probes into space and place them in orbit) are all ballistic. No spaceplane has ever been built.

THROW-AWAY SPACE VEHICLES

The first launch vehicles were not spaceplanes, but ballistic missiles converted for peaceful uses. Because of their purpose, ballistic missiles are designed to be used only once, so it follows that the first space launch vehicles were expendable. They were designed to carry out a specific task and to be junked afterwards. Spaceplanes, on the other hand, are naturally reusable, like aeroplanes.

This principle of expendability is unique in the history of transportation. All other forms of transport – cars, planes, trains, boats – are reusable. Expendability accounts for the high cost of early space flights: imagine building a jet to fly a crew across the Atlantic, having the crew parachute out near the destination and letting the aeroplane crash into the sea. The principle of expendability explains why it costs some $10,000,000 (£6,000,000) to put a tonne in orbit.

This seemingly extraordinary concept of throwaway space vehicles still prevails in the modern aerospace industry: today's launch vehicles are all ballistic and expendable, with the exception of part of the NASA Space Shuttle. Although the Orbiter – the upper stage – is reusable, the External Tank (see page 22) is expendable. The Solid Rocket Boosters – which provide most of the power for lift-off and the first two minutes of the flight – are jettisoned in the atmosphere and recovered at sea by parachute so that parts can be used again. This involves stripping them down and inspecting and re-

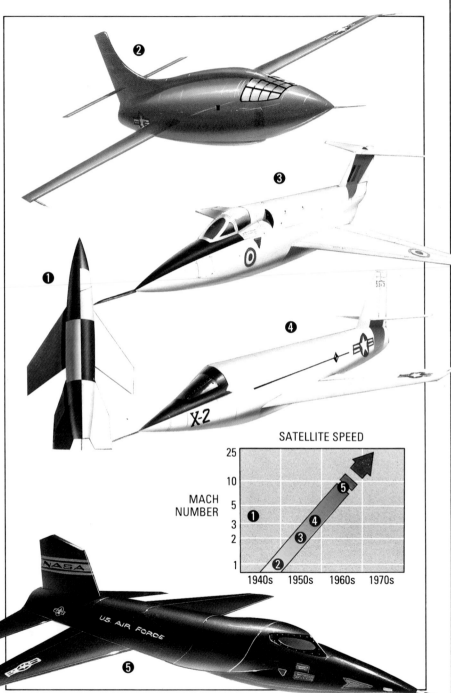

SATELLITE SPEED

MACH
NUMBER

25
10
5
3
2
1

1940s 1950s 1960s 1970s

The first rocket-powered aeroplanes were flown in Germany in the late nineteen-twenties. A thirties' design by an Austrian engineer, Eugene Sânger, for an aircraft that could fly nearly into orbit inspired much of the post-World War II work on winged vehicles carried out in Europe and in the USA, illustrated *left*:

❶

The winged version of the V-2 missile developed in Germany in 1945 was the first large winged supersonic flying machine.

❷

The American Bell X-1 was the first manned aeroplane to exceed the speed of sound, in 1947.

❸

The British SR.53 reached Mach 2.

❹

The Bell X-2 was the first aircraft to reach Mach 3, in 1956.

❺

The American X-15 first flew in 1959 and reached Mach 6.7 in 1967.

The speed graph of the record-breaking rocket aeroplanes (*left*) suggests that a successor to the X-15 could have reached orbital speed by about 1975.

❶

The X-15B was proposed in 1958 to succeed the successful X-15 high-speed research aircraft. It would have used the boosters designed for the Navaho to help it accelerate to satellite speed. With an estimated development cost of $88,000,000 (£55,000,000) the X-15B would have provided invaluable experience in the design of reusable aeroplanes able to fly into orbit at a bargain price.

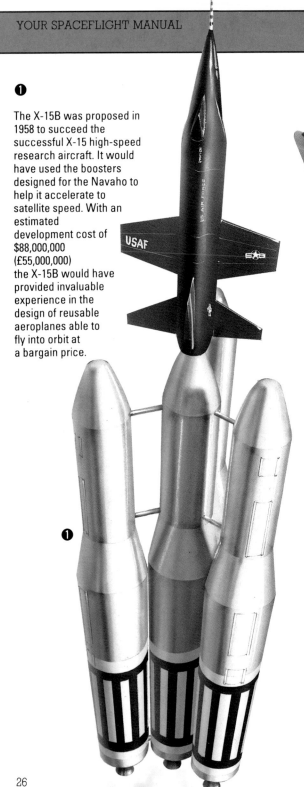

❷

pairing the metal parts, which are then added to the assembly line. Reusable boosters powered by liquid fuel could be cheaper because they would need no more than an inspection and refuelling after each flight. Thus the Space Shuttle is like a car which needs a new fuel tank and an engine strip-down and rebuild after every journey. Not very economical.

More than 30 years after the first satellite was launched, all launch vehicles are expendable, or largely so, and the government space agencies are stuck with the consequent high costs. They are also stuck with a high risk of failure since, for a number of reasons (explained in Chapter 4) expendable launchers cannot be made anything like as safe as vehicles which can be used many times.

Yet things need not have been like this. As early as the mid-nineteen-sixties all the ingredients were there for engineers to build a reusable spaceplane with which to explore beyond the Earth's atmosphere.

WHAT MIGHT HAVE BEEN

The 1945 winged V-2 (*see page 25*) demonstrated the feasibility of a flyback booster. A booster is the first stage of a launcher (a vehicle designed to launch a spacecraft into orbit); and a flyback booster is a conventional booster fitted with wings, a tail and landing-gear, so that it can be flown back to base after its flight, either by radio control or with a pilot on board. It can then be refuelled and used again.

Such a vehicle could have been built as early

❷

The X-20 Dyna-Soar was an early nineteen-sixties' American design for a manned spacecraft intended for research into aeroplanes which could fly at orbital speed. It was under construction when cancelled by the USAF in 1963.

❸

The Navaho was a long-range nuclear cruise missile notable for the use of a large booster stage. It never went into service and it was cancelled in 1957, but it pioneered much of the technology used by subsequent ballistic missiles and the space programme.

as the mid-nineteen-fifties: wings could have been fitted to a Redstone (*see page 23*), for example. Such a vehicle could have demonstrated the advantages of reusability and would have provided valuable working experience of the required technology. It would have been the logical first step in the development of a reusable spaceplane and would have greatly reduced costs. By the early nineteen-sixties the X-15 had flown higher and faster than a flyback booster, demonstrating beyond doubt the technology required for this very simple idea. Yet no flyback booster has yet been built.

In fact, between the nineteen-fifties and the nineteen-seventies some progress was made in the design of reusable spaceplanes. In the nineteen-sixties most of the major American and European aerospace companies had small project teams studying advanced launch vehicles. As a result of the success of the X-15 there was a consensus that a strong need existed for a reusable manned launch vehicle (a spaceplane) using X-15 technology, to ferry a crew to and from the new space stations then being planned. It would also have been used for launching small satellites and for servicing large ones. Incidentally, the tourism potential of space was also briefly considered at this time.

In the early nineteen-sixties the X-20 Dyna-Soar was designed (*see above, 2*). This was intended to be the first manned spacecraft with wings for recovery, but it was cancelled by the US Air Force in 1963 because of technical problems and lack of useful applications. By combining the experience gained from the

❸

design of this project with the experience of using liquid hydrogen fuel for the first time in the American Centaur upper stage of 1962, a fully-reusable launch vehicle could have been a fairly straightforward development. This could have been followed by a horizontal take-off space-plane by the middle of the nineteen-seventies: a successor to the X-15 capable of flying into orbit.

Several dozen projected designs for space-planes were around in the nineteen-sixties. Most were two-stage vehicles with horizontal take-off and landing, but other configurations were also studied. Perhaps the most promising design was the Dassault Aerospace Transporter project (*see right*); ('aerospace transporter' was the term in use in Europe at the time to describe a spaceplane).

The key to this concept was that the boost phase of the flight used both jet and rocket engines: the jets to take the vehicle up to supersonic speed and the rockets for accelera-tion to Mach 6, at which speed the upper stage would be separated. Other manufacturers prop-osed either all-rocket engines on the booster, and a very light (and therefore technically very difficult) structural design; or all-jet (air-breathing) engines, which would have necessi-tated the development of advanced new en-gines to enable the craft to reach the high separation speed necessary to give the orbiter a good flying start.

Had it been developed, the Dassault project would have entered service probably in the mid-nineteen-seventies as the first fully-reusable launch vehicle. The fact that it was reusable would have reduced launch costs considerably. This would have meant that it would be used more often; more frequent utilization would have lowered costs even more and led to even higher utilization, and so on, down a beneficial cost spiral. Eventually the operating costs of the project would have descended to the levels comparable with those of advanced aircraft.

The Dassault project would have been suit-able for carrying a few passengers. Had it been developed, a larger version could well be entering service by now and space tourism

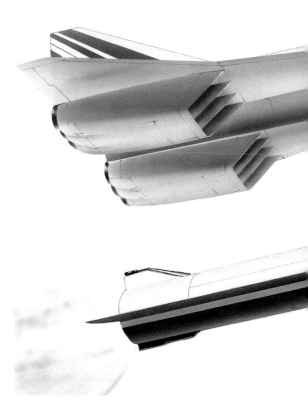

could be a reality today. As it is, much of the technology for the Dassault project has since been developed for other projects, notably Concorde, Ariane (*see page 44*), Spacelab and the Space Shuttle. Even now, 25 years later, it makes a great deal of sense to develop a reusable launch vehicle along the lines of the projects of the nineteen-sixties. Technically, this would now be a straightforward, state-of-the-art development.

POST MORTEM

Since all these projects were technically feasi-ble, why were they never built? Certainly, the reasons for not adopting a programme for the

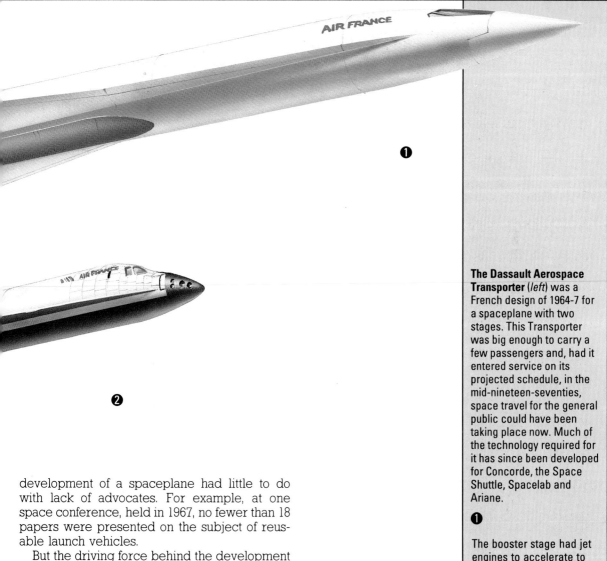

❷

The Dassault Aerospace Transporter (*left*) was a French design of 1964-7 for a spaceplane with two stages. This Transporter was big enough to carry a few passengers and, had it entered service on its projected schedule, in the mid-nineteen-seventies, space travel for the general public could have been taking place now. Much of the technology required for it has since been developed for Concorde, the Space Shuttle, Spacelab and Ariane.

❶

The booster stage had jet engines to accelerate to Mach 4.

❷

The orbiter had rocket engines which, utilizing fuel from the booster, accelerated the combined vehicle to Mach 6, the speed at which the booster would separate.

development of a spaceplane had little to do with lack of advocates. For example, at one space conference, held in 1967, no fewer than 18 papers were presented on the subject of reusable launch vehicles.

But the driving force behind the development of space technology during the nineteen-fifties was military. The USA needed to develop an intercontinental ballistic missile and spy satellites urgently. Then, during the nineteen-sixties, national prestige took over: priority was given to the race to the Moon. The development of flyback boosters would not have accelerated either of these two projects.

The first serious attempt to reduce launch costs came during the concept and pre-design phases of the Space Shuttle. NASA originally intended the Shuttle (*see page 23*) to be a fully reusable vehicle to support the operation of new permanent space stations. However, it was thought at the time to be necessary to attract support from the US Department of Defense, so the Shuttle was enlarged to carry the reconnaissance satellites then being launched by the Titan launch vehicle. As a result, the cost and risk of a fully-reusable design could not be afforded and the partially-expendable design was adopted.

In fact, because it is not fully reusable the hoped-for reductions in launch costs were not achieved and Titan has since been put back into production to launch the large reconnaissance satellites. Thus, from the point of view of the government agencies concerned, the need to reduce launch costs was not considered initially to be a priority; and later, when it was, the design was compromised by defence considerations. The Space Shuttle is, nonetheless, a magnificent achievement. It has performed very useful work; it has proved a vital piece of technology – thermal protection – needed for the development of fully-reusable launchers; and it could be developed into a very useful unmanned cargo launcher.

In parallel with the major programmes sponsored by government a commercial programme evolved for launching communications satellites. The high cost of launching them and the impossibility of repairing them in space made it essential that once launched, they should carry on working, and they rapidly became so reliable that only about 100 tonnes were required in orbit per year. The numbers launched were therefore insufficient to justify, in the short term at least, the development of a fully-reusable launcher for this programme.

When they were first seriously proposed in the nineteen-sixties, spaceplanes would have been difficult and expensive to develop. To recover the development funding on a strictly commercial basis would have required a long production run. This in turn would have required commercially credible predictions of large traffic levels. These were just not possible: there

was no mission requiring such traffic levels in the plannable future. Sub-orbital airliners were beyond the technology then available.

From a commercial point of view the development of a spaceplane will be economically feasible only for applications which will generate a large quantity of traffic into space every year. The first commercial use of space which could generate high enough traffic levels is likely to be space tourism: the making of short trips into orbit by fare-paying passengers.

This idea could not have become more than a speculative possibility until there had been enough experience of manned spaceflight to show that space travel can be attractive and safe, and that did not happen until quite recently. Flyback boosters leading to spaceplanes were not developed when they could have been.

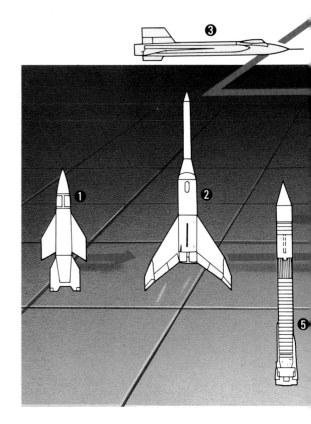

Government agencies were interested in short-term defence or prestige and the commercial demand was just not sufficient.

A decade has been lost. Had spaceplanes, instead of the Space Shuttle, been developed by government agencies in the nineteen-seventies, the cost of space operations would have fallen sharply in the nineteen-eighties and the possibility of fare-paying passengers visiting space would not seem far-fetched today. Indeed, the first such trips could well have taken place.

The diagram (*below*) shows a possible step-by-step approach to the goal of an aeroplane capable of flying into orbit, which might have taken place had space development been managed by people more determined to reduce costs.

 ❶

The winged V-2 of 1945 could have been developed into a flyback booster (a booster which can be flown back to base after its flight and used again) which would have greatly reduced launch costs.

 ❷

A flyback booster developed from the Redstone, for example, could have entered service in the mid-nineteen-fifties, ushering in an era of reusable, low-cost launch vehicles.

 ❸

The X-15 first flew in 1959, reaching a top speed of 4,520 mph (7,274 kph) in 1967 and zoom-climbing briefly into space. It inspired many subsequent spaceplane designs.

 ❹

The X-20 Dyna-Soar, designed in the early nineteen-sixties, was intended to be the first manned spacecraft with wings for recovery, but it was cancelled by the US Air Force in 1963 because of technical problems and lack of useful applications.

 ❺

The Centaur upper stage, an expendable launch vehicle built in 1962, used liquid hydrogen fuel for the first time.

 ❻

A fully-reusable launch vehicle could have been built by the late nineteen-sixties by combining the experience gained from the design of the X-15 and the X-20 Dyna-Soar with the experience of using liquid hydrogen fuel.

 ❼

A spaceplane, consisting of two stages and taking off horizontally, could have been built by the mid-nineteen-seventies: a successor to the X-15 capable of flying into orbit.

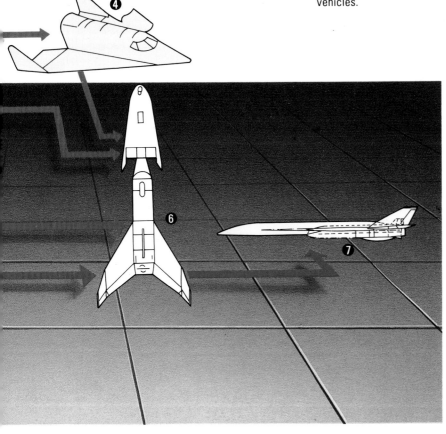

THE TECHNOLOGY

3

Seasoned space travellers in the year 3000 may be driven into orbit along an inclined ramp built from Earth into space. Alternatively, they might simply step into a lift at an aerospace terminal and be winched into space. A future Jacob's ladder would use the principle that a satellite orbiting the Earth at a height greater than 22,000 miles (35,000 kilometres) would exert a pull on a cable connecting it to a point on the Earth's Equator. If the satellite were heavy enough and the cable light and strong enough, it could be used to transport an elevator.

These aren't such daft ideas for the next millennium. Both ramp and elevator would have to be built of materials of a strength that has in fact already been realized, though so far only in microscopic laboratory samples. Such devices could reduce the energy costs of orbital transport to little more than $1,000 (£600) per tonne, about 10,000 times less than the cost of launching satellites today.

But these are ideas of the future. Back in the nineteen-nineties, space tourism has yet to be accepted by governments as a viable goal; a date for the first tourist spaceflight is far from being set; and the first spaceliner has yet to be built. However, the technical problems are straightforward: the basic principles are understood and, as Chapter 2 explains, much of the pioneering engineering work was done more than 25 years ago. What we have to do now is make it evolve.

FIRST PRINCIPLES

The first vehicle capable of reaching space – the V-2 ballistic missile (*see right*) – demonstrates the essential simplicity of the principles behind

Hermes, seen in this photograph (*left*) docked to a Columbus free-flier platform, is a three-seat manned spacecraft being studied by the European Space Agency. Full development is scheduled to start in 1991 for a first flight in 1998. Hermes will be launched into orbit by Ariane, a space launch vehicle designed to be used only once. We think that a fully-reusable launch vehicle – a spaceplane along the lines of the nineteen-sixties' projects – would be a much better project in which to invest. It would cost far less per flight and could cost less to develop.

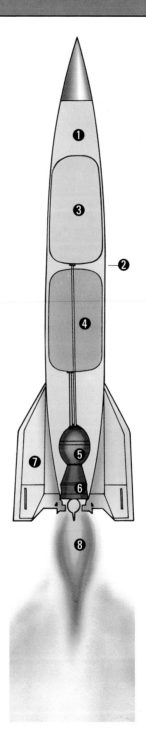

The V-2 ballistic missile (*left*) demonstrates the principles behind today's launch vehicles. The V-2 had no wings. It was kept up by the thrust of the rocket motor and, after burn-out (70 secs after blast-off, when all the propellant had been used), it simply returned to Earth on its unpowered parabolic trajectory, reaching a height of 60 mls (96 km).

Chamber housing warhead ❶

Body, long and streamlined to reduce drag at supersonic speeds ❷

Oxidant tank holding liquid oxygen ❸

Fuel tank holding alcohol diluted with water ❹

Rocket motor consisting of pumps, a combustion chamber and a nozzle ❺

Nozzle, through which hot gases under high pressure accelerate out of the motor at high speed ❻

Fins, for stability ❼

Exhaust stream, consisting of hot gas leaving the motor at high speed ❽ the design of a rocket-propelled spacecraft. The V-2's body was long and streamlined to reduce drag at supersonic speeds. At the top was the warhead; beneath it, taking up most of the internal volume, were the tanks holding the propellants. Both – fuel and oxidant – were pumped into the rocket motor, where they burned together to produce hot gas at high pressure. The high pressure forced the gas to accelerate through the nozzle and leave the motor at high speed.

This is the principle on which rockets work: the reaction to the acceleration of gas exhaust produces the thrust. You can try a simple experiment on reaction by sitting in a chair with castors – an office chair or a wheelchair – and throwing a heavy object, such as a brick or a book, away from you. The force on your arm as you accelerate the book reacts through your body to the chair, which will accelerate in the opposite direction. The thrust is simply the mass of the book (or hot gas) thrown within a given period of time, multiplied by the velocity at which the book (or gas) is thrown.

The V-2's thrust (56,000 pounds/25,000 kilograms) was greater than its weight (28,000 pounds or 13,000 kilograms), so the vehicle accelerated upwards. After 70 seconds all the propellant had been burned and the V-2 was moving at 3,500 miles per hour (5,600 kilometres per hour), or about one-fifth of satellite speed. Before burn-out the missile turned over to a pre-selected angle from the vertical, depending on the required distance to the point of impact. It was now unpowered and in very thin air, and followed more or less the trajectory of a large stone thrown at the same height and speed. It then re-entered the thicker layers of the atmosphere and fell to the target detonation area.

SPEEDING INTO ORBIT

The V-2 was a big step towards a spaceliner: it could reach space. At an altitude of 60 miles (96 kilometres) – the maximum height the V-2 reached – the air has about one-millionth the density at sea level, so the V-2 can be considered to have been in space for a brief period. But there was still a major breakthrough to be made: reaching orbit. The main obstacle to this was the amount of fuel required.

Propellant took up 75 per cent of the V-2's take-off weight, enabling it to achieve a maximum speed of 3,500 miles per hour (5,600 kilometres per hour), only one-fifth of the velocity needed to go into orbit. Most of the work from the engine was used to accelerate the V-2 to high speed, some was needed to overcome the drag of the atmosphere, and some to support the weight of the vehicle. In free space, away from drag and gravity, a V-2 would reach a speed of 6,300 miles per hour (10,000 kilometres per hour).

But to reach orbit an object must accelerate to a speed of about 17,500 miles per hour (28,000 kilometres per hour, called satellite speed or orbital velocity) in a horizontal direction; and it must reach an altitude of more than 100 miles (160 kilometres), in order to be clear of the atmosphere. It is far easier to launch a spacecraft to reach satellite height than satellite speed. If you threw a ball upwards from the ground at 4,000 miles per hour (6,400 kilometres per hour) and there were no air resistance, it would reach a maximum height of 100 miles (160 kilometres) before falling back to Earth about six minutes later. This is less than a quarter of the speed needed to sustain a satellite in orbit, and it requires less than one-sixteenth of the energy (which is proportional to the speed squared).

In order to reach orbit a V-2 would have to be filled with propellant up to as much as 98 per cent of its take-off weight, leaving only 2 per cent for everything else. Clearly, this is not practical. A propellant weight of around 85 per cent is a practical upper limit for a space vehicle consisting of just a propellant tank, a rocket engine and payload. With V-2 engines such a vehicle would have a maximum speed of only about 6,000 miles per hour (9,600 kilometres per hour) or about one-third of satellite speed.

One way of reducing the amount of fuel required would be to use jet engines instead of rockets. Jets take in oxygen from the air,

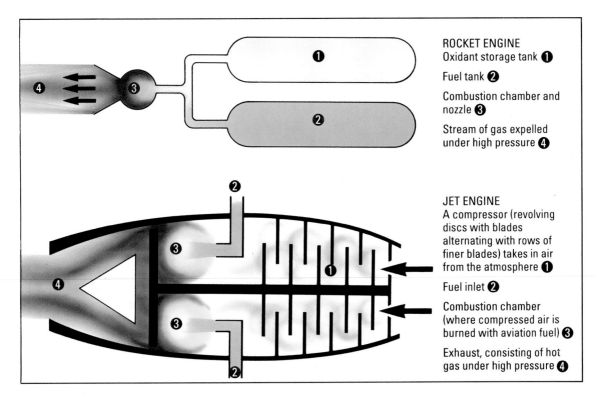

ROCKET ENGINE

Oxidant storage tank ❶

Fuel tank ❷

Combustion chamber and nozzle ❸

Stream of gas expelled under high pressure ❹

JET ENGINE

A compressor (revolving discs with blades alternating with rows of finer blades) takes in air from the atmosphere ❶

Fuel inlet ❷

Combustion chamber (where compressed air is burned with aviation fuel) ❸

Exhaust, consisting of hot gas under high pressure ❹

whereas rockets have to carry their own. Thus at low speeds jet engines produce 10 to 20 times more thrust than a rocket for the same fuel consumption. Unfortunately, at the time the first launchers were required, jets could operate only up to about one-tenth satellite speed, so they could not be used to solve the problem. Even now jets can only operate up to about one-sixth satellite speed. Aerodynamic heating and the difficulties of achieving stable combustion in a very fast air flow are among the problems remaining to be solved before jet engines can be made to operate at higher speeds. They are, of course, limited to altitudes at which there is an adequate supply of air, and cannot operate in space.

ONE STAGE OR MORE?

To build a vehicle that could achieve the speed required to put a satellite in orbit it therefore

In a rocket engine (*top*) an oxidizer from the oxidant tank, and a fuel such as liquid hydrogen from the fuel tank, are fed into the combustion chamber. They burn together, producing hot gas, which is forced by its pressure through a nozzle and expelled at a high velocity to produce thrust. Because they carry the oxidant they need, rocket engines can operate at any speed and height, including the thin upper atmosphere and in the vacuum of space. They are light and easy to install, but they have a high fuel consumption and, because they need to carry an oxidant as well as fuel, they have a high propellant weight.

A jet engine (*above*) has a large compressor at the front, which takes in air and feeds it into a combustion chamber, where it is burned with liquid kerosene or petroleum fuel. It is then accelerated at high pressure through a nozzle, driving turbines on the way, which rotate the compressor. Because it takes in oxygen from the atmosphere, a jet engine can produce about 20 times more thrust than a rocket engine for the same amount of fuel carried, but it cannot operate in the thin upper atmosphere and it cannot at present operate at more than about one-sixth of orbital-or satellite-speed, which is 17,500 mph or 28,000 kph.

became necessary to build a series of vehicles mounted on top of each other. Each stage of, for example, a four-stage vehicle will add about one-quarter of satellite speed to the velocity that has been achieved by the preceding stages. The payload (the satellite being transported) which is carried by the fourth stage and finally reaches orbit, is very light. The first satellite launched by the USA weighed just 18 pounds (8 kilograms): it was carried by the fourth stage of its Juno launch vehicle and weighed one four-thousandth of the vehicle's total weight.

The ratio of the weight of the fuel carried to the weight of the aircraft and its payload is known as the fuel fraction (*see opposite*). In the Juno and other launchers it amounted to typically 85 per cent on each stage, which allowed no weight to spare for devices such as wings, landing-gear, a cockpit or a pilot, which would have made recovery possible after the flight. This was one reason why early satellite launch vehicles could be used only once and were then abandoned. Another was that their design was based on ballistic missiles, which were expendable by nature of their task.

All this explains why early satellite launch vehicles were used for only one mission; why they consisted of multiple stages; and why they could carry only a very small payload. Modern launch vehicles have more efficient engines and can launch a heavier payload: typically as much as two per cent of their launch weight. However, some aspects of their design have not evolved substantially: they still consist of multiple stages and they are expendable. These are major reasons why the cost of space transportation has remained extremely high.

DESIGNING A SPACELINER

It would have been very difficult in 1904 to predict what the first airliners would be like. But this time around there are differences which can make it far easier to plan early spaceliners. First, the basic engineering requirement is fixed: to design an aeroplane which will accelerate to

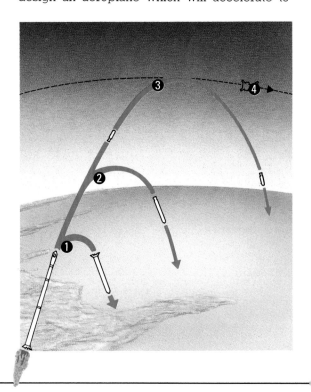

The 1960 Scout satellite launcher (*left*), like all launch vehicles built to date, is a multi-stage vehicle. The principle of staged launch vehicles (*right*) is that each stage accelerates itself plus the stages above it until it has used up its propellant, then separates and falls back to Earth, leaving the upper stages to accelerate on until satellite speed is reached.

The first stage (1) accelerates to a speed of 3,600 mph (5,760 kph), boosting the launcher to a height of 17 mls (27 km) within 83 secs, before separating.

The second stage (2) accelerates to 8,000 mph (12,800 kph) carrying itself and stages 3 and 4 to a height of 50 mls (80 km) in 130 secs.

The third stage (3) accelerates to 13,400 mph (21,440 kph), carrying itself and stage 4 to a height of 109 mls (175 km) within 171 secs.

The fourth stage (4) accelerates to satellite speed (17,500 mph or 28,000 kph), thus launching the payload, a satellite weighing typically 375 lbs (170 kg) into orbit at an altitude of, typically, 350 mls (560 km), 624 secs from blast-off.

The diagram (*far right*) shows the fuel fraction requirement for some of the vehicles mentioned in this chapter. (The fuel fraction is the ratio of the weight of the fuel carried to the total weight of the aircraft or launcher stage, including its payload). For an aeroplane taking off under its own power the highest practical fuel fraction is around 70%, rising to about 80% if it is air-launched. Thus, if existing engines are used, a spaceliner has to have two stages and to use liquid hydrogen fuel. Eventually very advanced jet engines will be able to operate fast enough to reduce the fuel to a level practical for a single-stage spaceplane.

1 STAGE (SSTO)			AIRCRAFT		2 STAGES	
98	87	80	72	45	86	64
EARLY ROCKET	LH$_2$ ROCKET	ROCKET PLUS AIR-BREATHING	RUTAN VOYAGER	747	EARLY ROCKET	LH$_2$ ROCKET

The highest fuel fraction ever achieved in an aeroplane was 72%. The aeroplane was the Rutan Voyager (*above*) a craft designed specifically to break the record for long-distance flight, by flying non-stop around the world without refuelling. The Rutan Voyager carried no passengers or cargo and was just strong enough and controllable enough to break the record. In 1986, piloted by its builders, Dick Rutan and Jeanna Yeager, it flew an officially-recorded distance of 24,986 mls (39,977.6 km). It beat handsomely the previous distance record of 12,532 mls (20.051 km) in a Boeing B-52H.

37

satellite speed. There were no such fixed requirements for early aircraft. Second, we know quite accurately the performance of the engines we will have to use. In the foreseeable future there is no substitute for rocket motors using liquid oxygen and liquid hydrogen propellants at least for the high-speed part of the flight to orbit. Pioneering aeroplane designers were faced with a bewildering choice of engines and propellers.

Running (operating) costs, scarcely a consideration for the pioneer aircraft designers, will be a crucial factor in the design of early spaceliners. Our review of the market in Chapter 1 shows that spaceliners would be used initially for ferrying staff and cargo to and from government-funded space stations; and then for space tourism. The breakthrough to operations approaching the scale of air travel will occur during the exclusive phase of space tourism development, when middle-income people can afford a trip to space after saving for a few years. This requires a price of around $10,000 (£6,000) per trip. To allow for indirect costs and profits, the direct operating costs (depreciation, crew, fuel and maintenance) of the spaceliner will have to be around half the fare at $5,000 ($3,000).

CONCORDE LOOKALIKE

From the various requirements considered above we can predict that a plane designed to fly passengers into space and back will be a high-speed airliner looking, superficially, much like Concorde. It will be able to take off from an ordinary runway; to get into space it will fly faster and higher until it reaches orbit. Because it will be flying at supersonic speeds a spaceliner, like a supersonic airliner, will be streamlined. It will be propelled through the early phase of the flight by jet engines; and accelerated into orbit by rocket engines, which will be fuelled by liquid hydrogen. This takes up to ten times the volume of the same weight of aviation fuel and it must be kept below its boiling point of -253°C, or only 20° above absolute zero. A spaceliner will also need a robust, durable and practical structure, containing accommodation for passengers, crew, baggage and some cargo.

In order to be certified to carry passengers, a spaceliner will have to pass full civil airliner standards of airworthiness. Various adjustments will have to be made to allow for flying into orbit – for instance, a spaceliner must not only protect the passengers from the intense cold of the upper atmosphere and outer space but also from the intense heat of re-entry into the atmosphere, typically over 1,000°C (2,440°F). Certification standards for civil airliners are must higher than those accepted for manned spaceflight.

A spaceliner designed according to the requirements outlined above will be a reusable, single-stage aeroplane, able to take off horizontally and using jet engines for the early part of the ascent. Many of the technical problems posed have been resolved, but some major developments must still be made, so such a vehicle must remain a long-term ideal. The first spaceliner to fly passengers into orbit will be a compromise between this ideal and what can be achieved using existing technology.

NEW TECHNOLOGY

A single-stage reusable spaceliner with a robust structure presents the designer with a problem: it must accommodate enough fuel to reach orbit in one stage. Using the most efficient rocket engines currently available – those fuelled by hydrogen – no less than 87 per cent of the take-off weight of a spaceliner would be taken up by the amount of propellant (hydrogen fuel plus oxidant) that would have to be carried, leaving only 13 per cent for structure, engines, landing-gear, furnishings, crew, passengers and baggage. This ratio of weight of fuel carried to the weight of the spacecraft and its payload is known as the fuel fraction. A fuel fraction as high as 87 per cent of take-off weight is clearly not practical when you consider that today's long-range airliners can take off with nearly 50 per cent of their weight as fuel.

The record fuel fraction for an aeroplane is 72 per cent, achieved by the Rutan Voyager (see page 37). The Voyager took off under its own power. An air-launched version, like the X-15 shown on page 18, could have carried more fuel and have achieved a fuel fraction of about 80 per cent. It is therefore unlikely that in the plannable future a single-stage spaceliner could achieve a fuel fraction much over 70 per cent, or that an air-launched (two-stage) spaceliner much more than 80 per cent.

One practical solution to reduce the amount of fuel required would be to use jet engines for the early part of the ascent, and modern rocket engines from thereon into orbit. At present jets can only operate up to about one-sixth satellite speed. This would reduce the fuel required to about 80 per cent, which is still too high for a practical single-stage spaceliner.

The ideal solution to the problem is to develop air-breathing engines that will operate to much higher speeds. These will require less fuel than rockets and will eventually reduce to a practical level the fuel fraction required to reach orbit. However, the engineering problems involved in developing such engines are immense and practical sub-orbital air-breathing engines are at least 20 years away. The designer's problem is, then, to find an engine/vehicle combination which can achieve these fuel fractions using engines which exist today.

PRAGMATISM RULES

A spaceliner which fulfilled all the design requirements and which used air-breathing engines which could operate at the height and speed of which only rocket engines are presently capable is, therefore, an ideal at which aerospace engineers must aim. But this ideal spaceliner cannot be built for at least 20 years. Economic considerations demand the formulation of a practical, shorter-term solution which will meet the requirement for safe and reliable transportation to space stations, and which is practicable enough for use during the pioneering phase of space tourism (see page 10).

In engineering terms, this means that some of the more desirable airliner-like features of what

would be the ideal spaceliner will have to be given up to produce a practical orbital transport system as early as possible. Reusability and design for frequent flights are clearly essential. The use of jet engines (up to their maximum speed) and horizontal take-off are highly desirable. This leaves single-stage as the only design feature which can sensibly be given up.

Our solution to the problem, then, is this: if the requirement for a single-stage operation is relaxed and the use of two stages is accepted, the design of the spaceliner becomes far easier. If rocket engines are used, each stage requires a fuel fraction of about 65 per cent, which is far more achievable than the 87 per cent necessary for a rocket-powered, single-stage vehicle. The penalty of staging is increased cost, since two vehicles have to be built and operated instead of one. However, the benefits of reusability and high utilization mean that the costs will be far, far lower than for the existing expendable vehicles, and acceptable for the economic requirements of space tourism (see page 49 **Operating costs**).

In fact, it was fully understood as long ago as the nineteen-fifties that the least technically demanding way of achieving a fully-reusable, aeroplane-like launch vehicle – a spaceliner, essentially – is to have two stages and to use hydrogen fuel. There were numerous studies of such vehicles in the nineteen-sixties (see pages 26-27).

In the face of the perpetual problem of funding for major new developments, it seems logical that the next step should be a spaceliner designed for minimum development cost: one that makes the least possible use of advanced technology and the greatest use of existing technology; that will be as small as possible, while still being useful – able to transport essential supplies to a space station, for example. The first spaceliner might, therefore, be a vehicle designed for space station supply, with provision for eventual certification for carrying passengers.

Such a spaceliner would be less efficient than one using more advanced technology, but it could be developed sooner. And the sooner the better because, in our opinion, the earlier it can be put into service, the earlier the benefits of aeroplane-like space operations will be demonstrated and the sooner will the way be opened for more advanced versions of the craft.

With these considerations in mind, we have reviewed the dozens of proposals for fully reusable launch vehicles which have been put forward over the years, and we have concluded that the published concept which is best suited to the spaceliner proposal is one developed by the Dassault Company in 1964 (*see pages 28-29*). It was one of several so-called aerospace transporters (a spaceliner, in our terminology), studied in Europe and the USA at the time.

However, there have since been many developments in the required technology and other proposed vehicles had worthwhile features. We have therefore carried out a concept study of a vehicle which is essentially an updated version of the Dassault project. It uses some features from other vehicles and some proposed by us, and it is designed for minimum development cost by making the best use of the technology which has become available since aerospace transporters were first proposed. It is:

SPACECAB

Spacecab isn't an ideal spaceliner. On the contrary, it's a compromise between what's available and what would require time and investment to develop. Like the first airline owners, who, before the development of airliners, ferried their passengers in ex-World War I aircraft because they were available and cheap, the first space entrepreneurs will send pioneering passengers into space in a craft that is workable, safe and based on existing technology adapted to new purposes.

When you first see Spacecab taxiing out to the runway of Dallas Fort Worth or Charles de Gaulle you'll be surprised how small it is. It has been designed to carry a crew of two and six passengers on the trip of their lifetime out into space; or a crew of two and 750 kilograms (15 hundredweight) of cargo to a space station; or, of

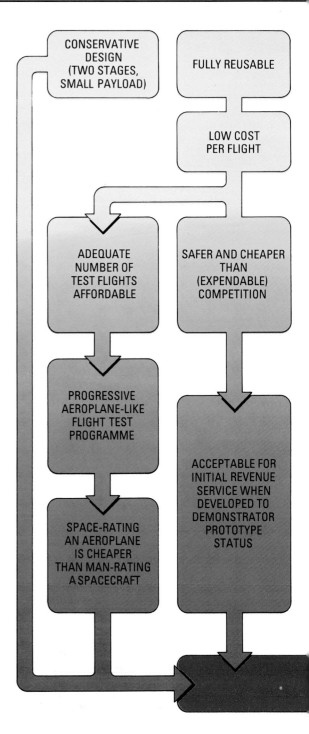

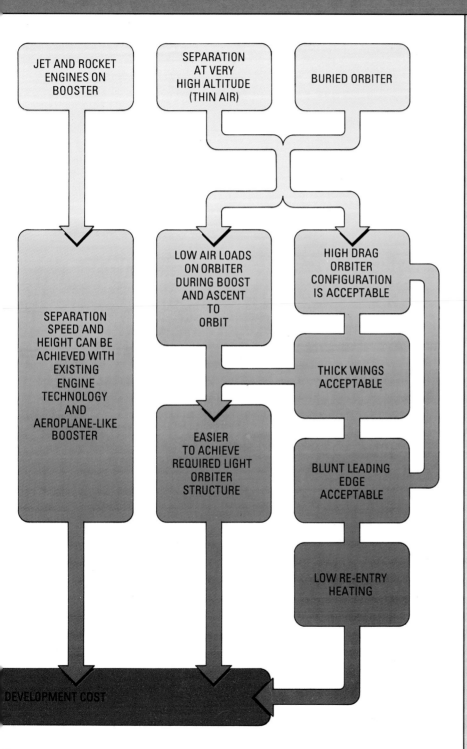

JET AND ROCKET
ENGINES ON
BOOSTER

SEPARATION
AT VERY
HIGH ALTITUDE
(THIN AIR)

BURIED ORBITER

SEPARATION
SPEED AND
HEIGHT CAN BE
ACHIEVED WITH
EXISTING
ENGINE
TECHNOLOGY
AND
AEROPLANE-LIKE
BOOSTER

LOW AIR LOADS
ON ORBITER
DURING BOOST
AND ASCENT
TO
ORBIT

HIGH DRAG
ORBITER
CONFIGURATION
IS ACCEPTABLE

THICK WINGS
ACCEPTABLE

EASIER
TO ACHIEVE
REQUIRED LIGHT
ORBITER
STRUCTURE

BLUNT LEADING
EDGE
ACCEPTABLE

LOW RE-ENTRY
HEATING

DEVELOPMENT COST

THE BRIEF
The basic requirements for the design of a spaceliner:

 1

A direct operating cost (depreciation, crew, fuel and maintenance), when in large-scale production, of about half the fare at $5,000 (£3,000) per seat, so that operators can cover their indirect costs and make a profit at a fare of $10,000.

 2

Design and certification to full civil airliner airworthiness standards.

 3

Moderate acceleration levels during boost and re-entry, for comfort.

 4

The ability to operate from existing airports with minimal new facilities.

5

Design to meet environmental requirements, such as noise.

The design features of Spacecab, are along the top of the diagram (*left*). The arrows and boxes show how they contribute to low development cost. The combined result of all these features, together with the important fact that Spacecab can be built using existing technology, mean that Spacecab's development should be not much more difficult than that of a prototype of a high-performance aeroplane.

41

course, some combination of the two. Its cabin is the size of a small business jet, the smallest useful size, we think, for a craft that will have to supply space stations. Its sweptback, streamlined shape, necessary for supersonic flight through the atmosphere, makes it look like Concorde, and in fact it's about the same size.

Our Spacecab is a new design, but the idea behind it has been around for some years. We have based it on the old European Aerospace Transporter projects, designed more than 20 years ago, updating them, of course, to take account of subsequent developments and the need for the lowest possible development cost.

We have been able to carry the design of Spacecab only as far as the concept stage. Going further would require a multi-million dollar feasibility study. Nevertheless, our conclusions will be sound because so much of the design is based on previous projects.

HOW SPACECAB WORKS

The Spacecab you will see on the runway may look just like a supersonic jet aircraft – but its appearance will be deceptive. From the outside you can see only about half of it: there's another spacecraft partly hidden inside. To be more specific, Spacecab consists of two stages: a booster stage and an orbiter stage.

The booster stage is a supersonic aeroplane, roughly the same size as Concorde. Four turbojet engines, of a type that have already been built, provide the power for take-off and acceleration to Mach 2. But in addition to these, two modified rocket engines (the Viking IV engine might be suitable) and associated fuel tanks are accommodated in the rear fuselage. These will accelerate the spacecraft from Mach 2 to Mach 4, the speed at which the orbiter will separate from the booster.

The orbiter's blunt, sweptback shape is dominated by the liquid hydrogen tanks, which make up about 65 per cent of its volume. Six Ariane third stage HM7 engines (or equivalent) provide propulsion. The payload bay consists of a two-person cockpit and a bay behind it with a

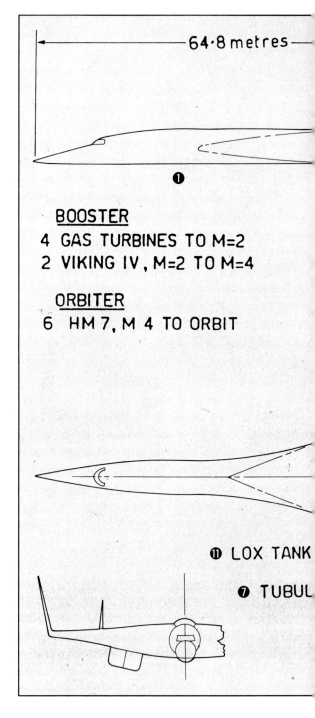

—64·8 metres—

❶

BOOSTER
4 GAS TURBINES TO M=2
2 VIKING IV, M=2 TO M=4

ORBITER
6 HM 7, M 4 TO ORBIT

⓫ LOX TANK

❼ TUBUL

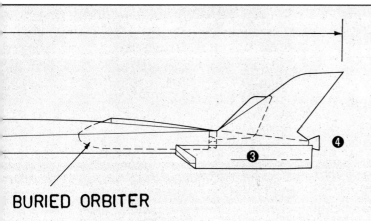

BURIED ORBITER

16·3 metres

CREW + 6 m³ PAYLOAD

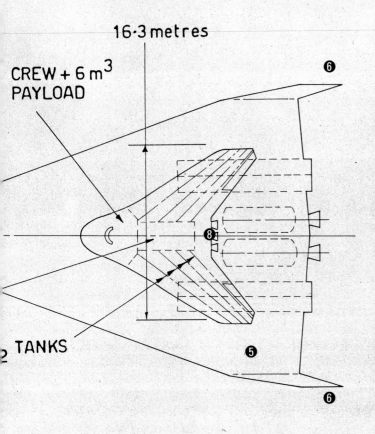

TANKS

Spacecab comprises two stages: a **booster** (**1**) and an **orbiter** (**2**). The orbiter is partly buried in the booster to protect it from air loads (the pressure on the skin from the airstream) during the boost phase of the flight to Mach 4 and to reduce the drag at supersonic speeds.

Four turbojet engines (**3**) provide the power for take-off, acceleration to Mach 2, flyback (following re-entry into the Earth's atmosphere) and landing.

Two rocket engines (**4**), such as the Viking IV, will accelerate the craft from Mach 2 to Mach 4, the speed at which the orbiter will separate from the booster.

A streamlined shape is essential to reduce drag at supersonic speeds, so the booster is long and slender, like Concorde, and has a pointed nose. The wings (**5**) are of the slender delta type for manageable trim change over a wide speed range. The booster and orbiter both have tip-mounted fins and rudders (**6**).

The orbiter has a blunt shape, since streamlining is not necessary for flight through space, but is sweptback to reduce heating during re-entry into the atmosphere. Liquid hydrogen (LH2) fuel is stored in tubular pressurized tanks (**7**) within its fat wings.

Six modified existing rocket engines (**8**) provide propulsion.

The cockpit (**9**) carries a crew of two. Behind it the **payload bay** (**10**) has a volume of 6 cu m (250 cu ft), equal to the cabin of a six-seater business jet.

In the **lox tank** (**11**), the Liquid OXygen component of the propellant is stored.

The **take-off weight** of spacecab is 181 tonnes.

useful volume of 6 cubic metres (8 cubic yards), the size of a six-seater business jet cabin.

The combined vehicle takes off from a conventional airport and climbs to Mach 2 using the turbo-jets only. At an altitude of 15 kilometres (just over 9 miles) the booster rocket motors are ignited and the vehicle accelerates to Mach 4 and pulls up to a high climb angle. At this point it is on a semi-ballistic trajectory (it's being more or less tossed into space, like a stone), and rapidly leaving the effective atmosphere at a climb angle of 40°. At this point its equivalent airspeed (the airspeed which at sea level would give the same air loads as in the thin air 40 kilometres or 25 miles up) is only 130 knots. This is low, equivalent to that of a light aircraft travelling at top speed. It has been chosen to keep the stresses on the orbiter, and the air loads during separation, to a minimum.

Shortly after the rocket motors of the booster have burned out (used up their fuel), the orbiter is raised clear of the booster on a linkage mechanism, its rocket motors are ignited, and separation takes place. The booster continues its unpowered zoom climb to a maximum altitude of 70 kilometres (45 miles). It then re-enters the atmosphere and is piloted back to base (using the jet engines), where it lands and is refuelled and prepared for the next flight. The orbiter, meanwhile, continues into orbit with its payload of passengers and/or supplies.

SPACECAB'S DESIGN

Compared with other projected launch vehicles Spacecab's two stages and modest payload constitute a conservative design. It is a strength of the concept that it involves no particularly difficult design problems and uses only state-of-the-art technology. Another strength is that Spacecab is fully reusable, which has the advan-

Ariane (*right*) is a European launch vehicle designed specifically to carry communications satellites. Its three stages are all expendable (they are transmuted into marine or space debris after their flight). Ariane was first launched in 1979 and has been very successful, with nearly half the market for commercial satellites.

tage of reducing the cost per flight very considerably compared with expendable or partly-reusable launch vehicles. A less obvious advantage of a reusable space vehicle is that, like an aircraft, it can be flight-tested progressively, starting with subsonic flights and working through supersonic, hypersonic and sub-orbital flights until orbit is achieved. So, even though it's a manned space vehicle, Spacecab can be test-flown for a certificate of airworthiness, just like an aeroplane. Moreover, reusable launch vehicles should be so much safer than expendable ones (*see Chapter 4*) that Spacecab could enter service carrying professional crews to space stations as early as the prototype stage of development, because even then it would be far safer than the partly-reusable vehicles it would replace, such as the Space Shuttle.

THE BOOSTER

As a first impression it may appear that the booster is a very advanced vehicle, since it is Concorde-sized, has a top speed of Mach 4, and can zoom-climb (describe a ballistic trajectory) to the fringe of space. However, the booster's flight envelope (its maximum speed at different heights) is well within that of the X-15, which flew more or less routinely to speeds in excess of Mach 4 more than 20 years ago and which achieved a maximum speed of Mach 6.7.

The boost phase lasts only a short time, so the aerodynamic efficiency, propulsive efficiency and structure weight of the booster are less important than for an airliner. Roughly speaking, if the drag of a long-range airliner is increased by ten per cent, the fuel requirement is increased by ten per cent. In the case of a booster, the fuel required is increased by only about three to five per cent, because most of the work done by the engines is to accelerate the vehicle rather than to overcome drag. As far as required efficiency is concerned, a booster can be compared to a dragster racing car, for which fuel consumption and endurance do not matter; and an airliner with a Le Mans racing car, where they do. A simple aerodynamic shape and structural design would therefore be adequate

initially, while providing scope for subsequent improvement. The booster has no long-range cruise requirement and its fuel fraction is less than that of Concorde. An ultra-light airframe is therefore not required.

The flight time above Mach 2 is very short, so exposure to severe aerodynamic heating is also short. A thin layer of insulation over the critical areas, such as the leading edges of the wings, should therefore provide adequate protection for a conventional light alloy structure. This technique is used to protect the less hot parts of the Space Shuttle orbiter, which nonetheless get far hotter than the Spacecab booster. Advanced new material and fabrication techniques are therefore not required.

ENGINES

Having both jet and rocket engines on the booster gives Spacecab the best of both. Air-breathing (jet) engines need much less fuel than rocket engines, but they are heavier. The engines in use as we write can operate only up to about one-sixth of satellite speed, and at altitudes low enough to give an adequate supply of air. An air-breathing booster can therefore achieve separation at only a modest speed and height, leaving the orbiter with a great deal of speed and height to gain before reaching orbit.

Rockets are lighter and easier to install, and can operate at any speed and height. However, they have a very high fuel consumption. A rocket booster can therefore offer a higher separation speed, but requires a high fuel fraction. A vehicle with a high fuel fraction would need a very light structure and lightweight systems.

Spacecab's engines will not have to be especially designed; engines currently in production can be used, but they will need modification for longer life and for use on manned vehicles. The jet engines are used up to the maximum speed currently obtainable with off-the-shelf units; the rocket engines then accelerate to separation speed. The jet engines are also used for flying to base and to airfields for maintenance and other purposes.

continued on page 48

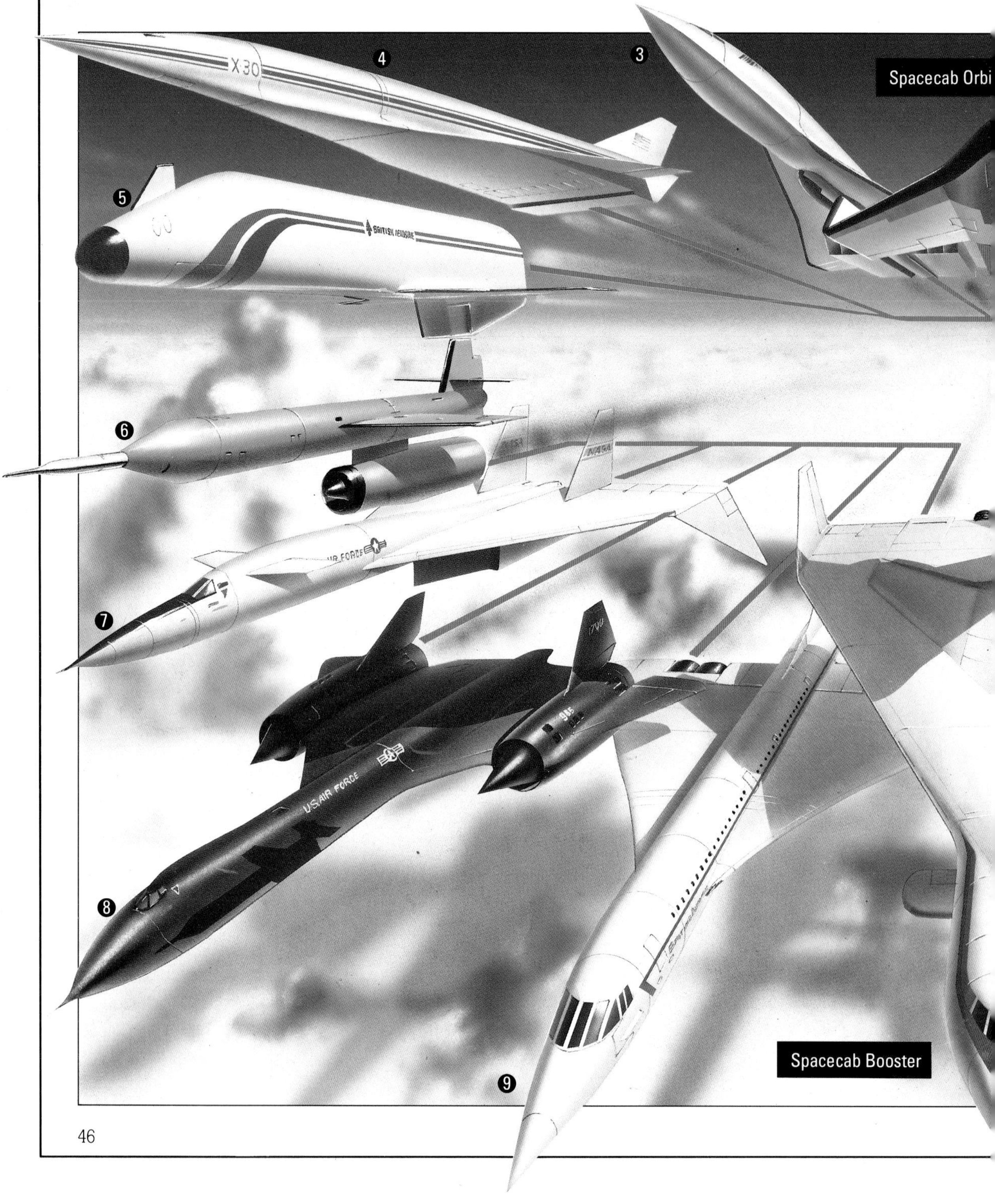

X30

4

3

Spacecab Orbi

5

British Aerospace

6

NASA

US AIR FORCE

7

US AIR FORCE

8

Spacecab Booster

9

46

The design of Spacecab is far from revolutionary. Most of the technical problems its development might have posed have already been solved on the real or projected aeroplanes and spacecraft in the illustration (*left*) during the period from 1938 to 1986.

SPACECAB ORBITER

ORBITAL SYSTEMS
Gemini ❶
Space Shuttle ❷

RE-ENTRY HEATING
Space Shuttle ❷

LIGHT STRUCTURE
1960s Aerospace Transporter ❸
X-30 ❹
Hotol ❺

SPACECAB BOOSTER

JET PROPULSION TO MACH 2
X-7 ❻
B-70 ❼
SR71 ❽
Concorde ❾

FUEL FRACTION
Concorde ❾

SEPARATION
Short-Mayo Composite ❿

ROCKET PROPULSION TO MACH 4
X-15 ⓫

The booster will require small control rockets to enable it to manoeuvre at very high altitudes, where aerodynamic control surfaces, such as rudders and ailerons, are ineffective.

SEPARATION

During the rocket-powered part of the boost phase Spacecab pulls up into a steep climb. When the rocket motors have used up their fuel the speed has reached Mach 4, the climb angle 40°, and the altitude 40 kilometres (25 miles). Because separation takes place in this very thin air, the air loads will be low and a simple link mechanism will be adequate to lift the orbiter clear of the booster.

From its position at separation the orbiter can accelerate to orbit without need of aerodynamic lift. It is kept up by the 'ski-jump' effect of separating at a high climb angle long enough for it to be able to accelerate to satellite speed before gravity pulls it back into the atmosphere. The 'ski-jump' is the name of a device fitted to the light aircraft carriers of the Royal Navy. Sea Harrier fighters are catapulted along the deck of the carrier and pushed up into the air by an inclined ramp at the bow (front) of the ship. This gives the engines crucial extra seconds in which to accelerate the aeroplane to flying speed, and enables it to take off at a heavier weight. As applied to Spacebus, the term refers to the upward kick imparted by the booster to the orbiter on separation. Because the orbiter does not need lift on the way to orbit, it can accelerate through very thin air, thereby reducing the air pressure on the skin and making a light structure feasible.

THE ORBITER

Since it has jet engines, the booster does have to fly fast and low when the air loads are high. However, the orbiter is largely protected from these loads by being partly buried in the booster. This, together with the ski jump separation (which enables it to accelerate to orbit in very thin air) permits it to have a very blunt shape, which reduces the weight of the structure and reduces the heating during re-entry.

The orbiter needs a light structural design because of the requirement for a very high fuel fraction of 83 per cent. This is higher than is necessary for an 'ideal' two-stage design, but we have chosen to keep the separation speed low so that the booster can be built like a robust aeroplane using existing technology. The solution we propose is to carry the propellant in pressure-stabilized (inflatable) tanks, which also form the basic wing structure. These pressure-stabilized wing tanks are not a new idea. They were proposed for several of the nineteen-sixties' spaceplane projects. None has yet been built, however. The lightest ballistic missile propellant tanks – those of Atlas and Blue Streak – were inflatable, but they did not have to act as wings as well.

Structure weight fractions even lower than those of the Spacecab orbiter are required by proposed single-stage-to-orbit (SSTO) vehicles, such as Hotol and the US National Aerospace Plane, because they have similar fuel fractions, but heavier (air-breathing) engines. Moreover, their structures have to be designed for much higher equivalent air speeds, typically 600 knots as compared with 300 knots. (SSTO vehicles have to fly at high speed under their own power through the lower levels of the atmosphere; the Spacecab orbiter is carried through them.) If these proposed SSTO structures are on the margins of feasibility, that of the Spacecab orbiter should be well within them.

Most of the technology required for the orbiter has been developed for previous aeroplanes or spacecraft (*see pages 24-25* and *46-47*). It uses existing rocket engines, modified for longer life. It does not have to fly on the way up, so there are no difficult aerodynamic problems. Heating on re-entry will be less severe than on the Space Shuttle, because Spacecab has a lower wing-loading (weight per unit of wing area), and can re-enter higher in thinner air, where the heating is less intensive. The low wing-loading results from carrying the hydrogen fuel internally rather than in a separate external tank.

Hydrogen fuel is so bulky that the tanks

carrying it have to be large. In the Spacecab orbiter the wings double as hydrogen fuel storage tanks, and these present the designers with one new problem to solve: the design of these combined wing/fuel tanks, which must be very light. The fact that the orbiter's wings avoid high air loads during the ascent to orbit helps, but a lighter structure than has yet been achieved on an aeroplane is still required.

Orbiter systems, such as those for navigation, communications, attitude control, rendezvous and docking, life support, power and environmental control were developed for the NASA Gemini of 1965. Much of the work done on Hermes could also be applied to Spacecab.

Thus, Spacecab should present its builder with straightforward engineering problems. As a result of careful choice of design features, and using existing technology where possible, there is only one aspect of Spacecab that will require a research programme: the orbiter structure. Even that uses techniques proposed 20 years ago and is a less demanding design than is required by several present-day proposals.

SPACEBUS

Having developed a small-scale spaceliner to act as an effective stopgap between the existing hardware and the ideal spaceliner of the future, the need for a larger and more mature version would be the natural next step. Following Spacecab on our drawing board is Spacebus, its successor, designed to take the development of space tourism one step on: into its glamorous second phase.

Technically speaking, Spacebus is very similar to Spacecab. It is larger, like an airliner compared with a business jet. Its technology will evolve naturally from that of Spacecab. The larger cabin will be able to carry 50 passengers for the short journey time to a space hotel. Alternatively some of the seats could be replaced by a viewing room for passengers and a small zero-gravity gym (*see page 87*) for longer trips of up to ten hours, when passengers do not stay in a space hotel.

To improve overall efficiency Spacebus uses jet engines to a higher speed – Mach 4 instead of Mach 2. Mach 4 was chosen because it is about the fastest which can be achieved with existing technology, although the engine will have to be a new design.

OPERATING COST

After it has been in production for a few years and the builders and operators have become familiar with it and taken out the bugs – when it has reached maturity, in other words – Spacebus will cost about four times as much per flight as a Boeing 747 on a long flight: some $250,000 (£150,000) as compared with $60,000 (£36,000). The depreciation will be higher because Spacebus is more complicated and will cost more to build. Crew, insurance and maintenance costs will likewise be higher per flying hour but this is more than compensated for by the short flight time: ten hours for a long 747 flight compared with fewer than two hours for a Spacebus round trip to a space hotel. The biggest difference is the fuel cost, which is some six times greater for Spacebus. This is because Spacebus uses about twice as much fuel and because liquid hydrogen is very expensive.

Spacebus carries fewer passengers than the 747 – 50 compared with, typically, 400 – and so the cost per passenger is far higher: some $5,000 (£3,000) compared with $150 (£90). When the indirect costs are added on, the fare to orbit in Spacebus when it has achieved maturity (after about five years in operation, *see page 56*) will approach $10,000 (£6,000) per passenger. This is far more expensive than a flight in a 747, but acceptable for the second, exclusive phase of space tourism development (*see pages 10-11*).

The cost per flight of Spacebus may be more than that of a 747 but it is nonetheless some 1,000 times less than the Space Shuttle: $250,000 (£150,000) as compared with over $300 million (£180 million). This is achieved with more or less existing technology, by reusability and by operating like an airliner. So drastic are the financial penalties of using expendable launch vehicles.

SPACEBUS CONCEPT

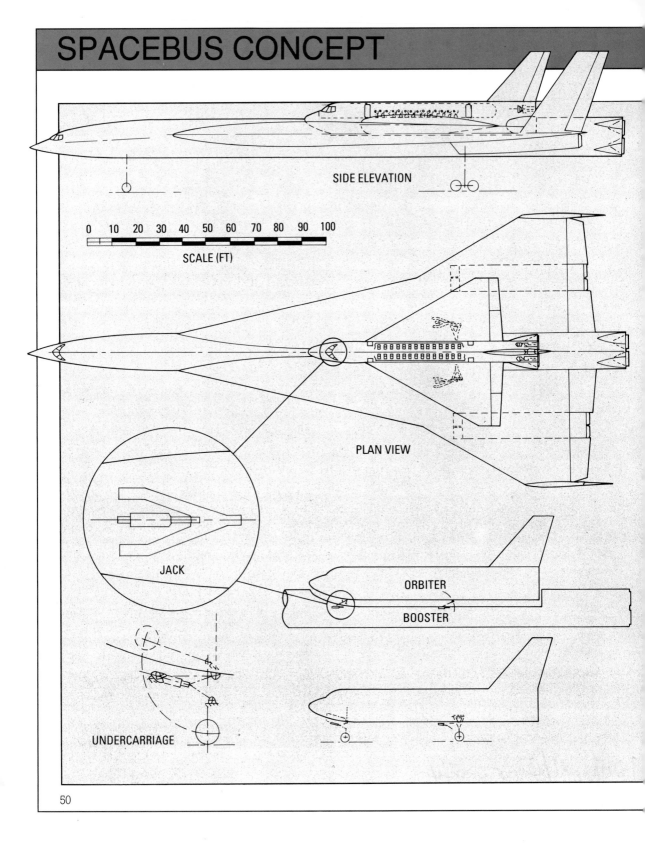

SIDE ELEVATION

0 10 20 30 40 50 60 70 80 90 100

SCALE (FT)

PLAN VIEW

JACK

ORBITER

BOOSTER

UNDERCARRIAGE

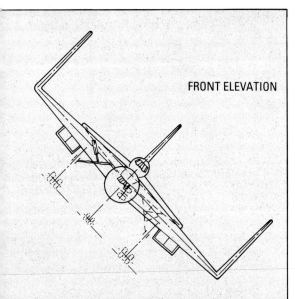

FRONT ELEVATION

Spacebus (*below*) is a larger, more mature version of Spacecab, our proposal for the first spaceliner, and it is scheduled to take over during the exclusive phase of space tourism development. Its general layout is much the same as that of its predecessor, but the orbiter fuselage has been stretched to accommodate up to 50 passengers. The maximum speed of the jet engines on the booster has been increased from Mach 2 to Mach 4 to reduce overall fuel consumption.

FACTS ABOUT SPACEBUS

Cruising speed (for positioning flights, etc): 550 mph	
Maximum speed (satellite speed): 17,500 mph (28,000 kph)	
No. of crew:	4 (2 in orbiter; 2 in booster)
No. of passengers:	up to 50

Booster		Orbiter	
Wingspan:	38 m (126 ft)	Wingspan:	21 m (70 ft)
Length:	88 m (290 ft)	Length:	34 m (112 ft)

Booster	Orbiter
Weight:	Weight:
Empty 130 tonnes	Empty 19.9 tonnes
Fuel	Fuel 84.7 tonnes
Fuel consumption	Payload
to Mach 4 64 tonnes	(50 passengers) 5.4 tonnes
Mach 4 to M6 64 tonnes	
flyback 32 tonnes	Total 110 tonnes
total: 160 tonnes	
Payload (orbiter) 110 tonnes	
Total 400 tonnes	

The cost comparison chart (*below*) shows that when mature, Spacebus will cost about four times as much as a long flight on a Boeing 747. It carries one-tenth the number of passengers, so the fare will be far higher, about $10,000 per passenger. This should, however, be acceptable for the second, exclusive phase of space tourism.

$0	$100,000	$200,000

COST PER FLIGHT

SPACEBUS
(MATURE)

BOEING 747

- ▩ DEPRECIATION
- ▩ CREW, INSURANCE, MAINTENANCE
- ▩ FUEL

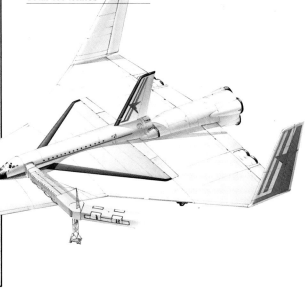

HOTELS IN ORBIT

Space hotels are, in effect, space stations in low Earth orbit, incorporating the facilities required for the accommodation and entertainment of passengers. Since the main justification for the early development of a spaceliner is the provision of safe and economical transportation for crews to and from space stations, by the time the mature phase of space travel development is reached, when space hotels will be needed for people wanting to spend a few days in space, the design, transportation, building and regular supply and maintenance of space stations will have reached an advanced stage; and the transition from space station to space hotel will be an easy one.

Several approaches to the development of space hotels are possible. One would be to build a hotel follow-on to the forthcoming NASA space station, Freedom, scheduled to enter service in the later nineteen-nineties. However Freedom is far larger and more elaborate than is needed for an early space hotel. Another route would be to cancel Freedom and replace it with a smaller station based on Skylab, which was operated successfully in the early nineteen-seventies.

The main Skylab structure was a converted third stage of the Saturn 5 launch vehicle used for the Apollo Moonflights. This vehicle is no longer available, but the Shuttle's External Tank,

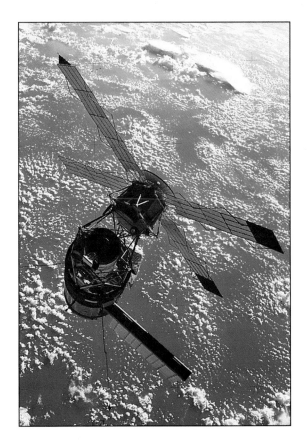

The US Skylab space station (*top right*) launched in 1973, demonstrated the essential features of a simple space hotel. The main structure was a converted third stage of the Saturn 5 launch vehicle used for the Apollo Moonflights. It had a usable volume of around 10,000 cu ft (295 cu m), which is roughly equivalent to the volume of two railway carriages. It orbited the Earth every 90 minutes at a height of 270 mls (430 km). Three teams of three astronauts each spent up to three months on board in 1973 to 1974, carrying out valuable scientific research and solving many of the basic problems of living in space. Perhaps most important for space tourism, despite the problems of an excessively pressing work schedule, the crews had a thoroughly good time up there.

Mir, the Soviet space station complex which was launched in 1986, is seen in orbit in this photograph (*bottom right*), taken from an approaching spacecraft. Up to six spacecraft can dock with this space station simultaneously.

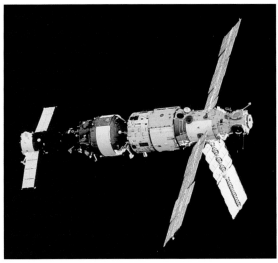

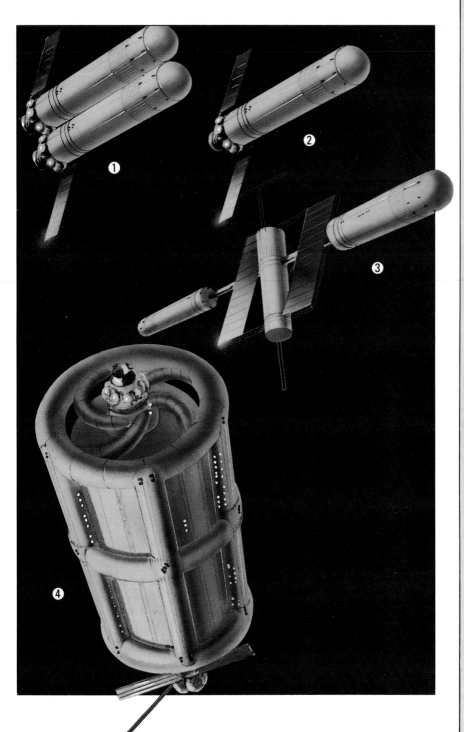

The development of space hotels (*left*) could be a straightforward process:

Stage 1: a simple prototype space station, based on the Skylab design but with a structure based on the Space Shuttle's External Tank. It has about twice the volume of Skylab and is still in production (a twin-tank configuration proposed by the US company, ETCO, is shown in the picture *far left*).

Stage 2: an 'auxiliary accommodation module' (*centre left*), which has a similar structure, but has additional safety features, such as shielding to protect against space debris and solar radiation, and features such as large windows, which make it attractive to passengers. Spaceliners would fly up and remain attached to it for a few hours, while their passengers enjoy 'zero-gravity recreation' (experiencing weightlessness) and Earth-viewing in the accommodation module.

Possible stage 3: a larger structure (*above left*) composed of three External Tank modules.

Stage 4: a large, self-contained space hotel (*left*), built to last many years, with rotating sections to provide gravity-regulated accommodation (to avoid the problems associated with eating, sleeping, washing and so on under zero gravity).

which has about twice the volume of Skylab, is still in production and would make an excellent substitute. A space station based on this component would cost so much less than Freedom to build that several could be built for the same money, which would increase the effectiveness of the programme. As the first stage in the development of the space hotel it would be used for research and for testing the design for eventual use by passengers.

As a stepping stone to a space hotel, this first space station would be followed by an auxiliary accommodation module. Before a space station could be used for tourists additional safety features would be needed, such as shielding to protect against space debris and solar radiation (*see pages 62-63*), for example, and it would have to be thoroughly tested in orbit. (Safety factors are discussed in detail in Chapter 4). Features such as large windows through which the hotel guests would be able to view the Earth, would make it attractive to passengers. Spaceliners would dock and remain attached to the accommodation module to give the passengers a few hours to enjoy 'zero-gravity recreation' (weightlessness) and Earth-viewing. They would then be flown back to Earth in the spaceliner leaving the module unattended. Essential life-support services would be provided by the spaceliner, which would also be used for rapid evacuation in an emergency. Because the spaceliner would always be alongside while people were on board, the life-support systems of the auxiliary accommodation module would not have to be proven to such a high degree of reliability as for a self-contained space station.

The accommodation module could be available perhaps by the beginning of the second, exclusive, phase of space tourism development. A self-contained space hotel would be the third step. This would have artificial gravity for the comfort of guests. Eventually, very large hotels would be built with recreation facilities, such as areas in which guests will be able to fly and swim in low-gravity conditions. Such a hotel is described and illustrated in Chapter 5.

This development pattern is only one of several possible patterns. The main point for now is that space hotels involve no particularly difficult new technology. All the essential pioneering work has already been carried out, notably on Skylab.

What will a large space hotel look like? Chapter 5 illustrates one possible idea only. One advantage of a structure in orbit is that it is not subjected to the gravitational loads of earth-bound structures. The basic structural elements can therefore be very large and very light. Architects will be able to give their imaginations free rein, inventing new shapes to take advantage of the freedom from weight.

LAUNCHING A SPACE HOTEL

Large launch vehicles (called, technically, heavy-lift vehicles) will be needed to launch the space hotels. The larger hotels will need to be launched in modules and assembled in orbit. Launchers currently in production, such as the U.S. Space Shuttle (*see page 23*) and the European Ariane (*see page 44*), are capable of carrying small hotel modules to orbit. Both systems involve large, throwaway components, and the cost of sending a tonne into orbit is about $10,000,000 (£6,000,000). This is obviously too high for any sort of space tourism to be considered. However, new heavy-lift vehicles which offer a reduction in costs by a factor of ten are known to be feasible and will probably be developed for other purposes. As we write, one such vehicle, the United States Air Force Advanced Launch System (ALS), is scheduled to enter service in 1998. It will probably have reusable liquid fuel boosters. The stated aim of this project is to achieve launch costs of about ten per cent of those for the Space Shuttle. Even these cost levels, which work out at about $1,000,000 (£600,000) per tonne, are much higher than transportation costs on Earth. However, a space hotel has to be launched only once and it would be able to accommodate so many tourists during its useful life of ten years or more, that a cost of about $1,000,000 (£600,000) per tonne just

Heavy lift vehicles are large launch vehicles intended to place heavy payloads in orbit. The Soviet Energia, which launched the Soviet Space Shuttle (*left*) is currently the world's largest. The largest Western launcher was the Saturn V.

to transport the hotel into space is just bearable, at least during the exclusive phase of space tourism development.

Today's space stations are very expensive. This is basically due to the extremely high cost of launching them, and of sending crews to and from them, which forces a high-cost culture on to everything associated with them. The fact that the crew have to be fully-trained astronauts (you can't just send up plumbers or electricians to repair a breakdown) adds to the cost. On nineteen-nineties' budgets only one or two are financially possible and as this book goes to press there is only one, the Soviet Mir Station (*see page 52*), in orbit. The launch and operation of the existing space stations are accompanied by a blaze of publicity. Adverse publicity might have a devastating effect on the programme's continuation, so practically everything has to work right first time, particularly because evacuating in an emergency is very difficult.

TIMESCALE

Given the proposed development sequence: Spacecab first because, using existing technology, it is intended to be the quickest and cheapest to produce; Spacebus second, because it's the most advanced version that can be built in the medium term using more or less existing technology; and the ideal spaceliner, the long-term solution, requiring the development of new technology; it is possible to work out a timescale for the evolution of the first two phases of space tourism.

Given a fair wind – assuming, that is, that the development of space tourism becomes a major international objective in the early nineteen-nineties, and also that the development of spaceliners turns out to be as straightforward as we have suggested – the timescale could be very short. Spacecab prototypes could be used for space station supply (ferrying cargo and professional staff back and forth) and for servicing satellites within seven years of the starting date. Three years is a typical time for an advanced jet aeroplane to progress from go-ahead to first flight. Add one year to allow for the incorporation of Spacecab's new features; two years between now and go-ahead; and one year from first flight to early operations; and the total is seven years.

The prototypes would not be able to carry fare-paying passengers. In fact one of their functions would be to carry out a programme of test flights with the object of obtaining what will be the space equivalent of a Certificate of Airworthiness. This will be a protracted business: an airliner might require as many as 1,000 flights over a period of a year before obtaining a Certificate of Airworthiness; the certification of Spacecab would take longer, perhaps as many as three years. Once certified, Spacecab could be used for early pioneering tourist flights into space – so certification must surely mark the beginning of routine space transportation.

The granting of the first 'Certificate of Spaceworthiness' to a spaceplane will, therefore, be a milestone in the history of aeronautics. This major milestone could occur ten years from the start of the development of Spacecab. Until then, space will continue to be used by craft designed as government-funded projects for defence, prestige or scientific research, and for the very few commercial projects which are financially viable at a transportation cost of several million dollars per tonne. Developments thereafter will be driven by what the market – primarily the general public – wants.

Still assuming the earliest possible start, we project that the development of Spacebus would sensibly start after Spacecab had been designed, following a time-lag of perhaps two to five years, depending on the availability of the finance and the dictates of the market.

A new airliner approaches its design targets of reliability and maintainability after, typically, one or two years in service. Spacebus would take longer because it uses technology which, although available now for experimental purposes, has not yet been exposed to everyday airliner operations. The thermal protection sys-

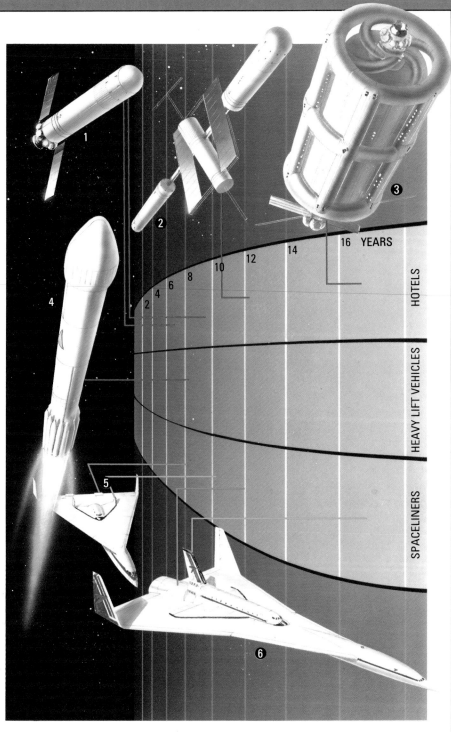

1

2

4

2

4

6

8

10

12

14

16 YEARS

5

6

HOTELS

HEAVY LIFT VEHICLES

SPACELINERS

THE TOURISM WAY TO SPACE

The development of space tourism could be rapid if it is given high priority. The timescale (*left*) assumes the earliest sensible start:

❶

A simple space station based on Skylab would be built in about seven years. A development suitable for use by passengers from Spacebus while docked alongside could follow about three years later.

❷

A self-contained space hotel could follow some two years later.

❸

A large hotel could follow in just under 20 years from the start of the programme.

❹

A new heavy lift vehicle for launching these spacecraft would take about eight years to develop.

❺

Spacecab could enter service in about seven years and given its 'Certificate of Spaceworthiness' about three years later.

❻

Spacebus could achieve its 'Certificate of Spaceworthiness' two years after Spacecab and could be approaching maturity some five years thereafter, about 17 years from the start of the programme.

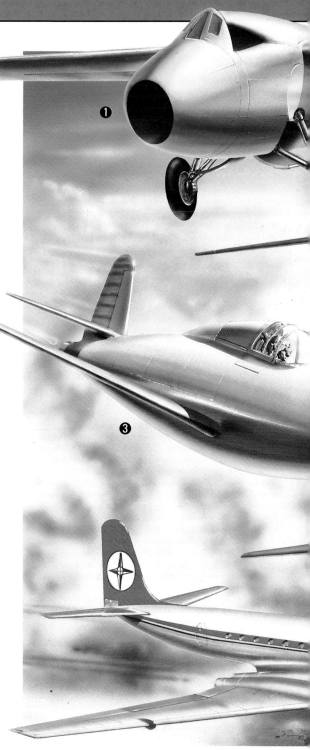

tem and the rocket motors are the two most obvious examples. A comparable example might be the eight years (1944 to 1952) it took jet engines to mature from early military operational flights to airliner service. With the benefit of the experience with much of the technology in the earlier Spacecab, Spacebus's technology could be approaching maturity after five years in service. Thus, in as few as 17 years from now Spacebus could have matured and be operating with a fare of $10,000 (£6,000).

The development of space hotels would follow in the wake of the spaceliner evolution. Although it is planned for other purposes (*see page 54 under* **Launching a space hotel**), the concurrent development of a new heavy-lift vehicle, such as the American Advanced Launch System, would facilitate the development of space hotels by reducing the cost of launching them.

Further expansion of space tourism and suborbital transport would require a more advanced vehicle than Spacebus, probably an enlarged version with advanced jet engines.

These timescales are very much a speculative best case for progress towards not only space tourism but mere space transportation as an everyday event. They assume that development timescales are not limited by the availability of funding (which is discussed in detail in Chapter 6); that spaceliners turn out to be as straightforward to develop as we suggest; and that the public responds enthusiastically to the prospect of visiting space.

If the space industry set itself the target of granting the first 'Certificate of Spaceworthiness' within ten years from the start of the development of Spacecab, it is still just possible that the first tourists could fly out to space before the end of the millennium. This would be a fitting way of ending a century of breathtaking aerospace development and a spectacular start to the next millennium of human achievement.

The first pure jet aeroplane to fly was the Heinkel He 178 which first flew in August 1939. It was closely followed by the Gloster E29/39 in 1940. The first jets to enter service were the Gloster Meteor and the Messerschmitt Me 262 fighters, in the summer of 1944. A vast effort was poured into the development of jet engines in the years following World War II, and they were mature enough by 1952 to power the world's first jet airliner to enter service: the de Havilland Comet. Thus jets took eight years to mature from early military operations to airline service. We are suggesting that Spacecab could trigger a similar effort in spaceplane development, by demonstrating that airline operations to space are possible, and that Spacebus could be approaching its mature fare level of $10,000 (£6,000) per seat about five years after entering service.

❶ Heinkel He 178
❷ Messerschmitt Me 262
❸ Gloster E29/39
❹ Gloster Meteor
❺ de Havilland Comet

THE SAFETY FACTORS

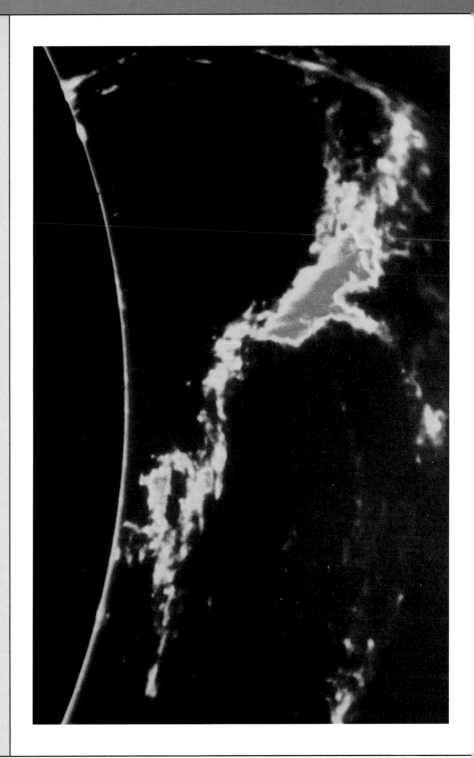

The idea of a trip into space sounds exciting, you may think, and talk about developing a space-liner very convincing. But perhaps you suspect, deep down, that when it comes to it space travel is really going to be far too expensive – and dangerous – for anything like that to happen in your lifetime. Your great-grandchild will be able to visit space, even your grandchild, but surely not you.

Such misgivings would be entirely justified. Right now space travel is indeed far too dangerous and expensive for the general public. The American and Soviet manned space programmes have together had three fatal accidents in just over 100 space flights. By contrast, commercial scheduled airlines aver-age about 1,000,000 flights per fatal accident. And as far as cost is concerned the cargo hold of the Space Shuttle has sufficient volume to carry a module of about 70 seats; so with a cost per flight of some $300 million (£180 million) each passenger would have to pay in excess of $4 million (£2.5 million) for a ticket.

What we're arguing is that the high risks and high costs of manned spaceflight can be overcome by quite straightforward develop-ments in engineering: instead of blasting you off into space in some kind of passenger-carrying ballistic missile, which, because it's essentially disposable can never be made safe or economi-cal, we propose to fly you up there in a reusable spaceliner, which can be made as safe as an airliner and much more economical to run than the Space Shuttle.

Solar flares (*left*) cause a sudden increase in radiation from the Sun, which, it was once thought, might affect Concorde, flying at, typically 17,000 m (55,000 ft) altitude, 3,000 m (10,000 ft) higher than subsonic jets. To avoid any danger to the health of its passengers it is fitted with radiation meters to detect unusually intense solar radiation. If this occurs the pilot could descend to a lower altitude and continue at subsonic speed. Solar flares of the magnitude to have such an effect are, luckily, rare, so as we write no Concorde pilot has yet needed to use this technique. No special radiation shielding is therefore thought to be necessary for launch vehicles or spaceliners, but space hotels will require layers of protection against such hazards.

SAFETY

We can state with reasonable certainty that touring space will become at least as safe as touring Earth. Spaceliners and space hotels will have to be designed and tested to meet stringent safety requirements. The certification authorities – the Federal Aviation Administration in the USA and the Civil Aviation Authority in the UK, or perhaps a new international authority governing orbital and sub-orbital transport – will need to be satisfied that their requirements are fully met before any spaceliner can take off with passengers or any space hotel admit guests. Spaceliners will have to be tested to meet all the specifications of airworthiness required of an airliner, plus additional requirements to cover operations in space. Space hotels will have to be tested as stringently, but tests governing the need to endure long periods of space orbit might replace those governing flying and landing in bad weather, for instance.

HAZARDS IN SPACE

There are, however, two hazards to which craft out in space are particularly susceptible, which will require special investigation: space debris and solar radiation. Space debris is a general term given to the many particles drifting in space which are not major recognized heavenly bodies, such as planets, moons, stars, comets and so on. It derives from two main sources: meteorites issuing from the depths of the solar system; and the remains of man-made satellites and rockets which have collided or exploded. It is a depressing fact that after only 30 years in space more than half the debris in Earth orbit is man-made. Efforts are now being made to reduce the formation of new debris, which now poses a hazard because it can collide with a space vehicle and cause damage.

Radiation from the Sun is more intense in orbit than at the Earth's surface because the atmos-phere absorbs much of the radiation nearing the Earth. Solar radiation is spread over a wide range of wavelengths, some of which are

61

harmful to health. Its intensity may increase quite suddenly when solar flares occur (*see page 60*).

The intensity of debris and radiation has been considered to be so low that no special protection has been built into manned space-craft so far. However, just as airline passengers expect lower risks than test pilots, space tourists will expect the risks to be as low as can be achieved. Detailed engineering studies will be needed to assess what levels of protection will be required, but the general principles are clear.

The safety treatment of spaceliners and space hotels will be significantly different. While they are airborne, spaceliners will be treated exactly like airliners, with similar safety margins built into the design. The lightweight liquid hydrogen tanks will probably present the most difficult design problem from this point of view. Rocket motors have a far worse safety record than jets, but this is largely because they are far less mature: the total number of hours flown by rocket-powered aeroplanes constitute a minus-cule fraction of the total flown by jets. They are probably not inherently more hazardous.

Spaceliners will spend so little time in space that special protection against radiation and debris will probably not be required. In any case the weight of shielding would be prohibi-tive, at least for early spaceliners. Neither are they likely to need special evacuation facilities. In the event of a spaceliner getting stranded in space, another one would go to the rescue, carrying a special air lock/evacuation pipe which would fit into the spaceliner's docking

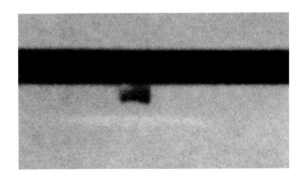

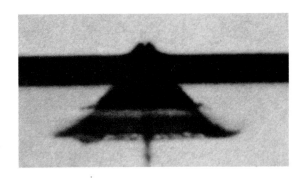

Microscopic space debris can have a devastating effect on the surface of spacecraft. The sequence of photographs (*right*) shows what happens when a polythene projectile of 8 mm diameter (far larger than the average particle of space debris) penetrates an aluminium plate 6 mm thick at 2,500 m (2,640 ft) per second. Photograph 1 (*top right*) shows the plate viewed end-on; the square image is the projectile. Photograph 3 shows the plume of debris on impact. Photograph 4 (*bottom right*), shows the penetration of the projectile. The diameter of the hole resulting in the plate is considerably larger than the diameter of the projectile. Experiments of this kind help engineers to select the type of shielding most suitable for a specific spacecraft.

The rescue ball is a ball made of fabric (*left*) or a plastic sphere (*above*) up to 39 in (1 m) in diameter, designed for emergency use by Space Shuttle crew who were not wearing space suits, and intended for use with a portable oxygen system. The crew member unpacks the ball and gets into it, straps on the oxygen system, puts the mask on and turns the system on. The astronaut then pulls the ball up over him or herself and gets a colleague to zip up the ball from the outside. A more sophisticated, self-sealing and self-inflating version of this simple device might be among the safety measures available in a space hotel in case of loss or contamination of the oxygen supply. Such devices would provide a safe environment in which to wait for a rescue craft.

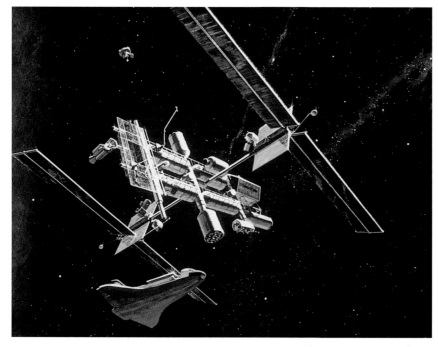

Spacecraft, present and planned such as the Space Shuttle and the forthcoming Freedom Space Station (one early configuration of which is shown in the illustration, *left*) have no special provision to protect astronauts against space debris or solar radiation. Tourists will expect safety standards as high as for earthbound tourism and shielding may well be needed for space hotels. Spaceliners will spend so little time in orbit that shielding will probably not be needed.

port. In case of depressurization, emergency air bags (*see page 63*) will be required.

Space hotels, by contrast, will spend so long in orbit that protection against debris and radiation will probably be required. Because they have to be launched just once, the weight penalty of the shielding can be afforded. A space hotel will have layered defences. Its orbit will avoid the worst debris and radiation belts. Its outer skin will keep out the background radiation and debris. Early-warning systems (such as radiation meters, radars and solar monitors) can be set to give early enough warning of particularly intense radiation or showers of debris to enable passengers and crew to move temporarily to one of a number of small, highly shielded areas, we have called citadels, within the hotel, where they will be safe until the hazard has subsided.

How to deal with loss or contamination of the air supply is one eventuality that will have to be thought out in advance. You can't breathe in a vacuum. One possible solution to this problem is to install detachable air-bags (*see page 63*) into the walls of rooms and passageways. If the air pressure falls below a certain point an alarm bell rings and you pull out a pack consisting of a plastic air-bag, which automatically starts to inflate as it emerges. You step inside and seal the opening. Inside it you're able to breathe.

These devices would provide life support until the crew were able to evacuate guests to undamaged parts of the hotel protected by a system of emergency air locks, or, in extreme cases, to other hotels or back to Earth in emergency 'lifecraft', the space equivalent of lifeboats. Until traffic levels justified specially-designed vehicles, lifecraft might be based on the Spacebus upper stage, with the rocket motors and rocket fuel tanks removed, as they would not be needed for flying back to Earth, and seats fitted in their place.

PERSPECTIVE ON STATISTICS

That's all very well, you may say, but what about the rockets that blew up or crashed? What about the Challenger tragedy in January 1986, when one of the solid fuel boosters broke away and burst the hydrogen tank a minute or so after take-off, which then exploded? A broad-brush comparison of the accident rates of various flying activities puts safety in perspective.

Commercial airliners on scheduled services currently achieve a fatal accident rate of around 1 per 1,000,000 flights. Private flying and parachute-jumping are about ten times more hazardous. High-performance military flying in peacetime is more hazardous still, by another factor of ten, since military pilots are often encouraged to approach the limits of both their aircraft's capabilities and their own. By contrast, commercial pilots are of course encouraged not to approach the limits of either.

The fatal accident rate for manned spacecraft has to date been as high as 1 per 30 flights, but the sample on which this statistic is based is small. American and Soviet astronauts have made about 100 manned spaceflights between them and there have been three fatal accidents during missions, one American and two Soviet. Thus, manned spaceflight has been about 100 times more hazardous so far than high perform-ance military flying and 10,000 times more hazardous than travel on a commercial airline.

The main reason for this high accident rate has been the use of launch vehicles with expendable stages for all spaceflights so far. American expendable launch vehicles had, on average, one major failure per 36 launches in the ten-year period in which the lowest number of accidents has been recorded to date, so expendable launch vehicles have a failure rate several orders of magnitude higher than that of any other type of transport.

Various factors combine to produce these results. Expendable launch vehicles have such a high cost per flight that the number of developmental test flights possible are, for financial reasons, typically as low as none or as few as two or three. Since a space launch vehicle can be flown once only, test flights of vehicles off the production line are impossible. For the same financial reasons, very few test

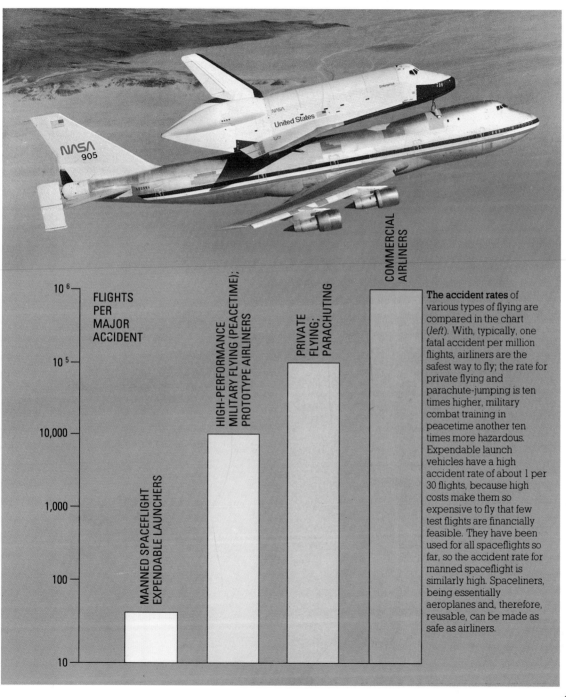

FLIGHTS
PER
MAJOR
ACCIDENT

10^6

10^5

10,000

1,000

100

10

MANNED SPACEFLIGHT
EXPENDABLE LAUNCHERS

HIGH-PERFORMANCE
MILITARY FLYING (PEACETIME);
PROTOTYPE AIRLINERS

PRIVATE
FLYING;
PARACHUTING

COMMERCIAL
AIRLINERS

The accident rates of various types of flying are compared in the chart (*left*). With, typically, one fatal accident per million flights, airliners are the safest way to fly; the rate for private flying and parachute-jumping is ten times higher, military combat training in peacetime another ten times more hazardous. Expendable launch vehicles have a high accident rate of about 1 per 30 flights, because high costs make them so expensive to fly that few test flights are financially feasible. They have been used for all spaceflights so far, so the accident rate for manned spaceflight is similarly high. Spaceliners, being essentially aeroplanes and, therefore, reusable, can be made as safe as airliners.

flights of the manned spacecraft they carry can be undertaken. The Space Shuttle, for example, was declared operational after the Orbiter had made only six spaceflights.

By contrast, an aeroplane under development undergoes about 1,000 test flights for its airworthiness certificate and each aircraft off the production line is given several test flights before entering service.

Expendable launch vehicles are so expensive that there is a strong financial incentive to squeeze in the last ounce of payload. This leads to a requirement to keep the vehicle weight to the absolute minimum, which in turn leads to low structural safety margins and to the lack of back-up systems. (In airliners, essential systems are duplicated, triplicated or even quadruplicated to enable them to carry on safely in the event of failure.)

Careful management can reduce the failure rate of expendable launch vehicles to about 1 per 100 launches: the failure rate of the most reliable satellite launch vehicles approaches this figure. But if you're thinking that 1 failure per 100 launches isn't too bad, think again. A rate of 1 crash per 100 air flights or car journeys would mean several air crashes per day at major airports, and most automobile owners would have a crash every few weeks.

There is just no way that large, complex launch vehicles designed for one flight only, filled with high-energy chemical propellants, can be made safe. Fully-reusable, winged, piloted launch vehicles are essentially aeroplanes and so can be tested thoroughly and made as safe as airliners, thus resolving the safety problem as well as the cost problem.

HEALTH AND COMFORT

There is no reason why anyone fit for travel on Earth should not be fit for a space holiday. Indeed, some physically handicapped people will find themselves as mobile in a weightless environment as the fully able-bodied; and the elderly may well rediscover the mobility they thought long lost. Inevitably some categories of people may be discouraged or even barred from travelling in space: the acceleration of take-off may prove harmful to people with a history of heart or blood disorders, and to pregnant women and babies. Indeed, it is possible that women in the later months of pregnancy would be excluded from travelling into space, since the specialized medical facilities required for premature or emergency delivery are unlikely to be available. Similarly, providing the kind of care required for severely handicapped people may be impracticable or too costly until a later stage.

There should be no real age limit, however: young children and healthy old people could look forward to a holiday in space. Sufferers from hay fever and other allergies caused by airborne particles may find relief because there will be no pollen or other irritants in the filtered and otherwise controlled and balanced air supply. Habitual or recurring back pain might diminish or disappear when the spine is relieved of the weight of the body pressing down upon it and its supporting muscles in zero-gravity conditions.

But weightlessness can have adverse effects. It can cause space sickness, for example, a kind of temporary nausea related to sea-sickness. Pre-flight medical screening will be routine, since susceptibility to space sickness could spoil an expensive holiday if untreated. Medication will contain this discomfort.

The experiences of cosmonauts indicates the possibility that several months of continuous weightlessness can cause certain complaints, such as muscular weakness, but these will not affect guests holidaying in space hotels for only a week or two. Moreover, the accommodation in space hotels will occupy rotating sections, built to provide areas of artificial gravity, so that everyday activities, such as eating, sleeping, washing and so on will be carried out in conditions as close as possible to the norm for the human body. Weightless recreation will take place in a large non-rotating section. Exposure to weightlessness can be kept below the limits found to be desirable for health.

During re-entry a spacecraft's speed falls from Mach 26 to subsonic. The photograph (*left*) shows a Space Shuttle model in a wind-tunnel re-entering the atmosphere, nose high so that it meets the air belly-first to slow it down. Air friction causes its outer skin to heat until it glows. To keep the temperature of the structure below 175°C (350°F) the resuable Orbiter has a lightweight thermal protection system, including thick, heat-reflecting tiles on the nose and belly able to withstand temperatures up to 1,275°C (2,300°F). New materials will be used to protect Spacebus, which re-enters the atmosphere higher up in thinner air, where the heating is less severe.

The outward flight up to orbit will inevitably involve higher acceleration than most people are used to, plus fairly rapid changes in acceleration. Some people could find this uncomfortable, but again, fairly simple preparation techniques can help passengers control these effects and make them bearable.

In fact pre-flight training will be an important and entertaining part of a trip into space, however short its duration. As a prospective passenger you may be encouraged to sign up for a few days in a space familiarization centre before your flight. Such centres will be full of fun fairground machines, such as big dippers and Ferris wheels, in which you will be able to practise building up your tolerance to varying gravity levels.

On the ground zero gravity can be sustained only for a second or two – during a dive from a high diving-board, for example, or going over the top in a big dipper, so familiarization rides in supersonic, rocket-powered aeroplanes, giving the sensation of weightlessness for a minute or two, will also be available as an optional part of pre-flight training. NASA has been using a KC-135 aeroplane (a military version of the old Boeing 707) to give trainee astronauts up to 25 seconds of weightlessness. In fact, in order to get to zero gravity as quickly as possible (to avoid wasting any of the precious 25 seconds) the changes in acceleration are higher than in a real launch, and they are repeated every two minutes; consequently, trainees call the KC-135 the 'Vomit Comet'. Don't be put off. This is far worse than anything you will be subjected to before or during your flight into orbit. Moreover, there are 20 more years of research into space sickness to go.

Once you're settled in your space hotel you can rest assured that there will be qualified medical personnel and facilities on board to look after minor medical emergencies. And any major emergency case can be evacuated back to Earth in an hour or so, either in the next scheduled spaceliner or, if necessary, in a lifecraft.

THE EXPERIENCE

5

We're going to assume that all the waiting's over. It's the year 2020. Since the nineteen-nineties, when you first heard that space travel could be a reality for everyone, not just for professional astronauts, you've been saving hard, determined to become a space tourist as soon as the prices dropped to a level you could afford.

The first commercial passenger spaceflights took place at the turn of the millennium – two decades ago – but only millionnaires could afford the novelty of those pioneering orbital flights. The first passengers had to travel out to a launch site at Cape York in northern Australia, near the Equator, because the launch vehicle could reach the orbits at the lowest inclinations only (*see page 71*). It was exciting but, looking back, all that expense and travel seems hardly to have been worthwhile just for a day trip.

Some people still trek out to that distant site for the launch, but now they do so from choice and perhaps a sense of history. New aerospaceports quickly opened: two in the USA, one on the East coast and one on the West; one in northern Japan; and one just outside Berlin. Eventually, the new, larger-capacity Spacebus began to replace the tiny Spacecab. Now the improved Mark 2 version is in service and there are several commercial fleets, so the costs of operating them have come right down. Sooner than anyone predicted, the price of a flight has fallen low enough for more and more ordinary people to afford the trip. Just a few years ago, following years of experiments with space-station derivatives, the first real space hotel opened to a fanfare of excited international newsflashes and headlines, and the first space holidaymakers

The Earth's curvature (*left*) will be clearly seen by guests in a space hotel orbiting at a height of about 300 mls (483 km), but the planet will still seem very close. Only the astronauts who flew to the Moon were far enough away to see it as a globe. In orbit, the curvature will be such that if you point to the opposite ends of the horizon the angle your arms make will measure 145°. Cumulonimbus clouds, black on the horizon, level off the top of the weather-making atmosphere in this photograph, which bears out Yuri Gagarin's observation that the sky is black and the Earth is a bluish colour. Dusk and sunset streak it a brilliant red – not once a day but every 90 minutes from the vantage point of Earth orbit.

spent three days and nights at a time in orbit.

More international aerospaceports have since opened: one in the Soviet Union, one as a separate aerospace facility on Charles de Gaulle Airport, just outside Paris; and one out in the British countryside near the coastal city of Bristol. So travellers can now choose from a growing chain of spaceports around the world, each of which handles several commercial spaceflights a day.

Of course, spaceflights are still pricier than supersonic flights on Concorde were last century – so the rich, the famous and the fashionable still pad out the passenger intake on most flights. Indeed, despite saving hard you were beginning to wonder whether you would ever be able to afford the price of a ticket until you were lucky enough to win one of the many competitions – with a week's space holiday as first prize – being offered by the international television stations. But spaceflight is so much more exciting than supersonic flight that more and more people are now signing up, as some of the other passengers on your flight did, on a savings scheme for a once-in-a-lifetime holiday in orbit.

PRE-FLIGHT TRAINING

However diverse may be the circumstances that brought you and your fellow passengers to this point, one thing is common to all of you: you will all have spent the past week in the Orbitours Travel Centre. There's now one attached to each of the major aerospaceports, including the new one close by. They're luxurious places, ideal for winding down from a stressful job, but their real function is to prepare guests for their spaceflight and their holiday in orbit.

By departure day you'll have learned so much about the procedure for getting into orbit and about life in an orbiting space hotel that you could write the Orbitours brochure. Through the panoramic window of the dining-room in the Travel Centre there's a mock-up of Spacebus: the craft that will soon fly you into space. From some angles it looks like an airliner, but you can see the two stages and, if you walk round the mock-up, the enormous rocket nozzles at the back, which tell you that Spacebus is very different from a jet airliner. For one thing, it flies about 30 times faster.

The Orbitours people are justifiably proud of their Spacebus fleet and want to show it off. They regale their guests with brochures the size of books giving the story of the craft. These tell you about the prolonged and sometimes dramatic fight to win acceptance not just for the design of a spaceliner but for the whole principle of space tourism. The brochures explain how Spacebus works; its shape; its rocket and jet engines; even its air supply and its electrical, sanitary and hydraulic systems. Despite the hype, you have to agree that Spacebus is an impressive vehicle.

In the Travel Centre you will have been given an audio-visual preview of what will happen minute by minute between leaving the Travel Centre and unpacking in your quarters in the space hotel. You'll be familiar with the space hotel before you get there: you'll have been told, for example, that even in the rotating section, where the passenger accommodation will be, you will weigh only a fraction of your weight on Earth; and your bathroom in the Travel Centre will be a replica of the one you'll be using in the space hotel.

Attending training sessions with your fellow passengers will have given you a chance to get to know them before the holiday starts. You'll have done weightlessness practice in an old widebody airliner flying a 'zerogee parabola' (a rapid ascent and dive, so the flight path of the aeroplane forms a parabolic curve); and run through emergency procedures with them. Maybe you'll have talked about some of the new space-sports you'll get a chance to try out when you're in residence 300 miles (480 kilometres) up. You might even have formed a study group to try to improve on your long-forgotten geography, so that you can recognize the Earth's continents and oceans, seas and deserts as they roll by beneath the windows of the hotel's viewing lounges.

You will have boarded Spacebus before the day of departure. Because anticipation of such a rare experience as flying into space is part of the pleasure, Orbitours will have arranged for talks and demonstrations to take place on board the craft, just for the fun of it. At some stage you'll be able to pre-familiarize yourself with the vehicle and its facilities. Giving you the opportunity to try everything out in normal gravity will be an important measure from the point of view of both comfort and safety. For the last part of the flight, and on arrival at the space hotel, you will be weightless and, despite the practice, this will be an unfamiliar experience. In fact, moving about in zero gravity is easier than perhaps it looks, provided you remember to do everything slowly and gently, giving your brain time to prepare for each move.

As well as the Spacebus mock-up you will have been able to go around a model of part of the space hotel, which has also been set up in the grounds of the Travel Centre. It isn't possible to simulate zero- and low-gravity conditions in a mock-up, but it will have given you a good idea of the hotel's general layout: the accommodation module where you will be living; the layout of the rooms; where the different facilities are; and so on. The real hotel is huge – the size of an aircraft hangar – so the mock-up represents only a part of it; from a distance it looks like a strange collection of tanks and pipes.

DEPARTURE

The space hotel's orbit determines when it passes over the aerospaceport, and the time your spaceflight is scheduled to dock will determine your 'launch window' – the period of time, whether day or night, when you take off. The diagram on page 71 explains why. If you travel in the morning you will be advised not to breakfast; if you travel later in the day you'll be advised not to drink anything for a while before take-off; and about an hour before the flight you will be given a diuretic to eliminate excess fluids from your body. This will help you adapt to zero gravity. Living on Earth, your heart has to pump your blood upwards against gravity, so when gravity disappears the blood is pumped too strongly. Unless you take these precautions you get a bloated feeling in your head.

If you packed a lot of gear for your trip you may be disappointed to find that most of your belongings will have to stay behind, locked up for safety in the Travel Centre. The weight of the spaceliner is critical in flight and each passenger will be able to take only a light travelling bag. You will be wearing a one-piece suit made of a synthetic material treated to increase its anti-static properties. For the early pioneering trips these were all supplied by the tour operator, and they're still available free, in various fabrics, styles and colours. They're functional garments, really, designed to be serviceable under conditions of zero gravity, so they have useful little features, such as pockets with Velcro covers, and Velcro patches on the backs of the thighs which you can use to anchor yourself to furniture when you need to.

But inevitably, as the fact of space tourism gripped everyone's attention, the fashion world focussed on this utilitarian dress, transforming it to the point where you simply couldn't be seen in the space hotel among all those music superstars, star designers, novelists and video personalities unless you were wearing designer spacewear created especially to hang around the Earth-viewing deck in, play space sports in and appear in at the essential Zee-Gee Space Discos.

And it's getting yourself up in your designer flightsuit and heading past the line of Travel Centre staff wishing you a good trip that really makes you feel you're on your way. You pass the press photographers trying to break through barriers to catch the celebrities in focus, and board the futuristic-looking shuttle bus waiting to take your party to the international aerospaceport. While you're waiting for the photocalls to finish you chat to one of the four Orbitours staff about the pros and cons of travelling to space on a regular basis and getting paid for it.

It's only a few minutes' ride in the spacious, air-conditioned shuttle bus before you disembark at the space terminal. Orbitours people lead the way and you're soon in the elegant VIP departure lounge, with its enormous, panoramic colour-print frieze showing one of the orbiting hotels being approached by a Spacebus, the beautiful blue and white orb of the Earth in the background. If you look carefully at the Earth you will see that the view from orbit is of the part of Europe where you are now standing.

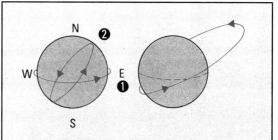

Ascent to orbit is usually to the east (*above left*), so that Spacebus travels in the direction of the Earth's spin. If it travelled in the opposite direction it would need more fuel to achieve orbital (satellite) speed. The position of the space hotel will determine which orbit Spacebus sets course for. The first space hotel is likely to follow an equatorial orbit (1), which is the easiest and so the cheapest to reach; and will probably be positioned at a low orbit at an altitude of as little as 10% of the Earth's radius. An equatorial orbit is the least interesting for the passengers, since from space you see only the Earth's equatorial regions. Orbits inclined to the Equator (2) are the most interesting. As the Earth turns below you, on successive orbits you see all of its regions up to the latitude of the orbit's inclination. From a 52° inclination, for example, you would be able to see London, Moscow and New Zealand. Unfortunately, however, inclined orbits are the most expensive to reach. Spacebus's successors might use elliptical orbits (*above right*), which would give passengers a view of the Earth from different distances.

SPACEBUS

Through one of the departure lounge's large windows you can see Spacebus standing in its taxi bay, ready for boarding. With its needle-like nose, its knife-edged wings and their raked tips, it looks the most streamlined vehicle ever. Beyond it you can see another stationed at its gate, surrounded by servicing vehicles, like worker bees around a queen: hydrogen and oxygen propellant trucks connected to the tanks that supply the rocket motors; an electricity generator truck topping up batteries; a truck replenishing the water supply; catering personnel going to and fro.

A flash of silver in the sun reveals another Spacebus outside a distant hangar, waiting for routine maintenance checks before the next flight. In the last ten years the international aerospaceports have become increasingly busy. Each one handles several commercial spaceflights a day, in addition to dozens of ordinary passenger aircraft operations.

It gets noisy in the departure lounge as the famous names on your flight give their videophone interviews. You scrutinize a picture of the Spacebus orbiter you'll soon be flying in. It looks the exact opposite of the booster stage – a short, blunt-nosed craft with great fat wings, looking as aerodynamically impossible as a bumble bee is said to be. But because it's a spacecraft it doesn't have to fly efficiently through air. The fat wings are good for carrying fuel and for slowing the craft in the atmosphere during the re-entry phase of the return trip to Earth. When joined to the booster stage, the orbiter fits into the rear of the fuselage, making so neat a contribution to Spacebus's elegant, swept lines that it's difficult, at first glance, to see there are two vehicles.

In the VIP lounge you're all asked to change your shoes for the soft-soled slipper-socks (all in luminous tones, this year, inspired, says the Designer of the Year 2020, by the hues of the Northern Lights seen from space) which attach to the ankles of your spacesuits. Your shoes seem almost the last link with Earth; relinquishing them reminds you that you won't be putting much weight on your feet for a few days.

A mating ramp is used to load the orbiter on to the booster. The orbiter is towed on to the ramp, the upper end of which is fitted over the booster. Sets of hydraulically-operated roller tracks then move the orbiter along the ramp and over the booster's rocket engine fairings until it slides into position over a pair of jacks built into the booster. As these jacks are operated the orbiter sinks down into the booster's delta wings, to form an integral part of Spacebus's streamlined shape.

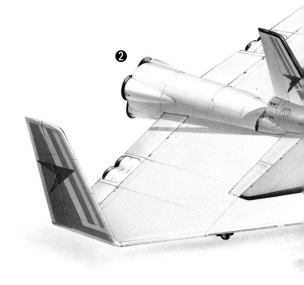

❷

FACILITIES
Closed-circuit TV broadcasts announcements and demonstrations of safety equipment and displays the views from the cockpit windows.

Stereo system attached to each seat, capable of reaching certain long-wave Earth stations and the space hotel radio.

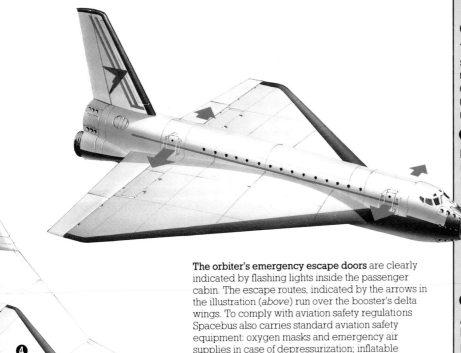

❶ The booster has a very streamlined shape: pointed nose and delta wings, in order to generate the minimum possible air resistance.

❷ Four powerful HM60 or J2S rocket engines take over from the four turbo- ramjet engines, beneath the delta wings, at an altitude of 15 mls (24 km), to power the booster to separation speed.

The orbiter's emergency escape doors are clearly indicated by flashing lights inside the passenger cabin. The escape routes, indicated by the arrows in the illustration (*above*) run over the booster's delta wings. To comply with aviation safety regulations Spacebus also carries standard aviation safety equipment: oxygen masks and emergency air supplies in case of depressurization; inflatable lifejackets and emergency medical supplies.

❸ A long jetway is set up before take-off for passengers boarding the orbiter. The emergency route follows the same path over the booster's delta wings.

❹ The orbiter fits into the booster's delta wings in order to maintain Spacecab's aerodynamic shape.

Pull-out video attached to each seat capable of receiving in-flight CCTV.

A space guide service is provided by the staff. A space tourist video is available.

The cabin staff are trained in first aid and the treatment of simple medical and psychological problems.

❺ The booster's cockpit houses a crew of two: the captain and the co-pilot.

73

TAKE-OFF

The call comes for space passengers to board. You take a last look through the lounge windows at Earth from ground level and instead catch sight of the boil-off from the waiting Spacebus – the cloud of vapour formed by the venting of a jet of ultra-cold liquid hydrogen from the fuel tanks in the wings.

Through the transparent walls of the jetway you walk through on your way into the craft, Spacebus fills your vision. You get an excellent view of both the orbiter and the booster. The passenger entrance is located towards the front of the orbiter, so you walk directly over the leading edge of the booster's starboard wing. You can see all the way back towards the great nozzles of the booster rocket engines. Looking down, you can also see where the orbiter's wings are set into the wings of the booster to protect them from the airstream and to maintain

the ultra-streamlined shape of the combined vehicle – essential for its high travelling speeds.

Each time you enter the cabin its loftiness strikes you. The ceiling of the new Mark II Spacebus is considerably higher than that of a passenger aircraft, so its interior doesn't have that claustrophobic feeling the inside of an airliner has. This was not possible on the less advanced Mark 1 Spacebus for weight reasons, so its cabin height was the same as on an airliner. The walls are padded and fitted with handholds. The staff lead you along the aisle to your seat. On the back of the seat in front is a Mach meter, a device which indicates the speed of the vehicle in terms of the speed of sound. It will tell you when the orbiter is reaching orbital speed, or 25 times the speed of sound, when the numbers climb towards Mach 25.

The strict 'no smoking' rule imposed on all

spacecraft, which carry hydrogen and oxygen propellants, is read out by the cabin staff during the run-through of the emergency drill. Before take-off the familiar 'Fasten Seat Belts' sign will light up, but you may need help. You'll have shoulder straps as well as a seat belt. The cabin door is closed and sealed. The staff go to their stations. The craft vibrates as the jet engines on the booster stage start up. There's a wait as the Captain requests the go-ahead to taxi.

You feel a slight jolt as the brakes are released and the vehicle begins to taxi to the runway. Because you're in an aerospaceport and not an airport you feel like a VIP. There's a familiar push in your back during the take-off run, as the vehicle accelerates down the runway. Then there's the pleasant floating feeling you get as the undercarriage breaks contact with the ground.

Spacebus's four powerful turbo-ramjet engines enable it to take off (at the same speed as Concorde: 250 mph or 450 kph) from the airport runways 2 mls (3 km) long, designed for long-haul jets.

Four HM60 or J2S rocket engines take over at Mach 4 to provide the thrust for acceleration to Mach 6, which takes Spacebus to separation speed. Between take-off and separation Spacebus flies 250 mls (450 km) over the Earth's surface.

Over the intercom the Captain welcomes you all and reminds you that there won't be any levelling out. Unlike an airliner, Spacebus will climb and accelerate more or less continuously right up to the space hotel's orbit. Almost incidentally during this fantastic climb, it travels 2,000 miles (3,200 kilometres) around the world.

Out of the window next to your seat you will see the view southwards along the Atlantic coast of France open up as the craft climbs towards its orbital destination. The view also flashes up live on a large video screen at the front of the cabin. As speed builds up – by the time the display on the Mach meter has reached Mach 4 – the clouds have been left behind.

The whistle of the jets gives way to a muffled roar as the booster rockets take over. Already Spacebus has climbed so high that the air is too thin for its jet engines to operate. The push in your back gradually increases as the craft accelerates and you are pulled down into your seat as the climb angle increases to 40°. The blue of the sky through your window deepens. Looking down, you see the South of France to your left, and then, as hundreds of miles slide by in just a few minutes, way past it into Spain as you head south. On the screen, the blue line of the horizon begins to curve as you climb high enough to see it as the rim of the Earth.

At about 100,000 feet (30,500 metres) you experience that magical moment when the sky changes colour from blue into the inky black of infinite space, from which the stars shine out brilliantly. Shortly afterwards the roar of the booster stage rocket engines stops, and, as the spacecraft continues to climb, your body floats up against the harness.

Directly after take-off Spacebus begins its climb into orbit (*top right*), accelerating from subsonic speed to Mach 4 in ten minutes. Using its four powerful turbojet engines, it climbs through the dense air up to 15 mls (24 km). At this point, about ten minutes after take-off, it changes to its rocket engines. Separation takes place one minute later at a speed of Mach 6. It accelerates to orbital speed and climbs towards the space hotel. The booster, separately piloted, drops back to Earth and flies back to the aerospaceport. The total time to reach orbit is just over 20 minutes.

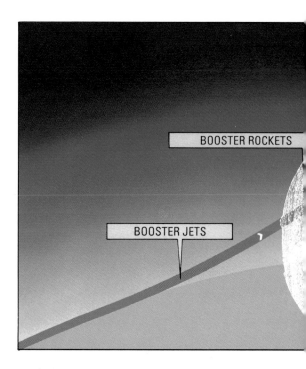

BOOSTER ROCKETS

BOOSTER JETS

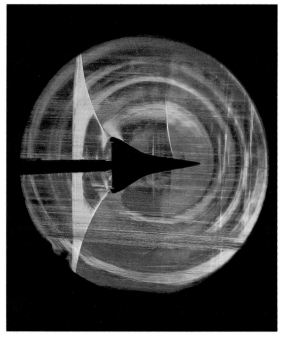

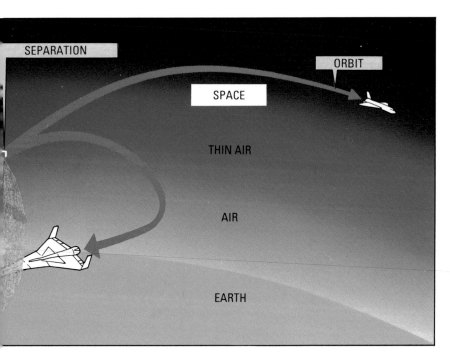

SEPARATION

ORBIT

SPACE

THIN AIR

AIR

EARTH

Like all supersonic aircraft Spacebus creates a sonic boom when it crosses the sound barrier. During subsonic flight the air can 'hear' an aeroplane coming because the craft sends out pressure waves in all directions. These give the molecules of air ahead time to, as it were, 'get out of the way' as the aircraft arrives, so the air flows smoothly over the surfaces of the nose, wings and tail. The boom occurs when the aircraft reaches the speed of sound (Mach 1). At this speed it is travelling too fast to give the air advance warning of its arrival, so it 'catches up' with the pressure waves, which pile up in front of the aircraft to form a shockwave (*left*).

The pressure across the shockwave rises rapidly, like the bow wave of a ship. It is swept back, like the ship's bow wave rippling to the shore. At the point where it reaches the ground it sounds like a whipcrack: the sonic boom. So, like Concorde, Spacebus may have to delay the supersonic phase of its flight until it is away from areas of human habitation, perhaps over the sea. The faster the aeroplane flies the more swept back is the shockwave, and at hypersonic speeds (above about Mach 5) it lies almost parallel with the aircraft's surface. This is called Newtonian flow.

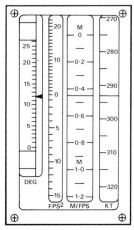

Spacebus lifts off at about the same speed as Concorde, about 250 mph (400 kph). As she climbs and accelerates, her speed in Mach number (the ratio of true airspeed to the local speed of sound) is displayed on a Mach meter (*below left*), fixed to the back of each passenger seat.

Mach 1 (the speed of sound), about 700 mph (1,100 kph) at an altitude of 20,000 ft (6 km).

Mach 4 is about 2,660 mph (4,300 kph) in the cold air at an altitude of 15 mls (24 km). (The speed of sound goes down as the temperature is reduced.)

Mach 6 is about 4,400 mph (7,000 kph) at 30 mls (48 km), the altitude at which the orbiter stage separates from the booster and continues the journey to space orbit.

At Mach 26, about 16,000 mph (26,000 kph) at about 60 mls (97 km) the orbiter can be said to have escaped from the Earth's atmosphere into space. It continues to climb and to accelerate to the speed and height of the space hotel (17,500 mph or 28,000 kph and 300 mls/480 km for early ones). When clear of the atmosphere there is no sound and Mach number ceases to be a useful measurement.

77

SEPARATION

There's a low rumbling sound as the hydraulic jacks raise the orbiter away from the booster; and a sudden roar as the orbiter's rocket engines burst into life. You feel a surge forwards as the booster drops away. On the video screen the image of the underlying Earth is crossed by the booster, its job done, being piloted away to head back to the spaceport. Meanwhile you head east over the Sahara Desert as the orbiter soars on up, carrying you with it.

The numbers on the Mach meter built into the back of the seat in front are now changing rapidly. You are glad of your pre-flight familiarization with high g (gravity) loads because the acceleration has now built up to a steady 1g, a bit too high for comfort, but necessary to keep down the fuel required to put Spacebus in orbit. As the fuel is used up, the orbiter races ever faster towards orbit. The numbers 7, 8, then 9 on the Mach meter give way to 15, 16 and 17, and continue to climb. Though you can see it's happening you may have a hard time believing it's possible to travel so fast. But you feel the relentless push in your back, accelerating and carrying you up more than 10 miles (16 kilometres) higher every minute. Because this high up there's no air resistance to slow the craft down, you eventually pass Mach 25 and the Captain may announce that you're now travelling ten times faster than a bullet. Then the engines cut out. There's a sudden silence.

The intercom crackles a formal welcome to Earth orbit: the first staging post for human journeying into the solar system and the threshold of humanity's greatest dreams.

The Captain announces that you're now almost in the same orbit as the space hotel you will be staying in and begins the series of manoeuvres necessary to rendezvous with it. This, you feel as you wait to catch your first glimpse of the hotel, was worth the two decades' wait.

Now the 'Fasten Seat Belts' sign goes off. An announcement comes over the intercom to inform you that you're now in zero gravity and to remind you of your training: remember to move gently if you decide to leave your seat'. Staff help you slide your seat back from the reclining

position (this was carefully calculated by the designers of the spacecraft to minimize your discomfort during the launch acceleration). Although it isn't strictly necessary, most passengers appreciate this opportunity to relax and enjoy their first views of the Earth from space as the pilot allows Spacebus to cruise slowly towards the hotel for an hour or so.

As the stewards and stewardesses move

Just as the Space Shuttle was tracked by a team of ground controllers (*above*), so will the progress of Spacebus be monitored from Aerospace Traffic Control Centres in space stations in high orbit. Aerospace Traffic Controllers maintain constant contact with the crew of Spacebus's booster stage and, after separation, with the orbiter crew.

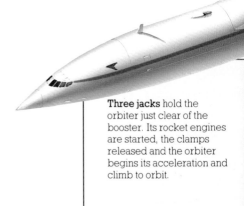

Three jacks hold the orbiter just clear of the booster. Its rocket engines are started, the clamps released and the orbiter begins its acceleration and climb to orbit.

around the cabin you can see why the Mark II Spacebus's ceiling is so much higher than an aircraft's: it gives more room for people to move about in zero gravity without getting in each other's way. You're just thinking about stretching your limbs when you're arrested by the sight of the space hotel coming into view around the darkened rim of the Earth, sparkling in the sunlight like an enormous jewel.

Separation takes place 11 minutes after take-off in the thin upper atmosphere at a speed of Mach 6 (*left*). At a height of 30 mls (48 km) the crew activate the jacks which keep the orbiter buried in the booster.

Jacks ❶

Orbiter ❷

Booster ❸

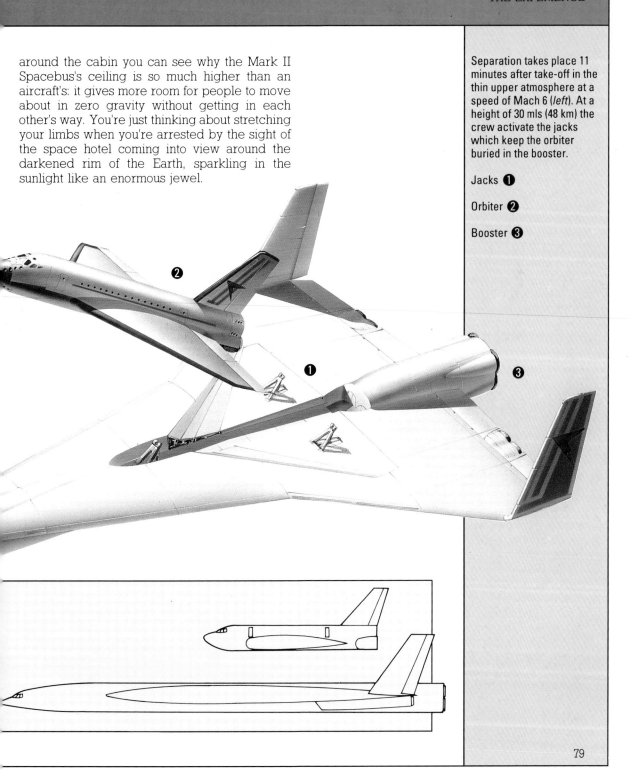

DOCKING

The Captain announces over the intercom that you have about half an hour before docking in which to enjoy the view. While he's talking a series of panels in the cabin roof slides back, to reveal a line of skylights. Each oval window is more than one metre (three feet) long. These windows are a recent improvement. Because of their weight they could not be fitted to early spaceliners.

You decide to take a closer look, so you undo your seat belt and find yourself floating up out of your seat. You look round for something to grab and find a handhold sited conveniently near your right hand. Once you've caught hold of it you feel less insecure and, remembering your training, you look over to where you want to go and push off very gently towards the ceiling. You tumble slowly as you move upwards, but a steward catches you by the arm and steadies you. Now you grip another handhold beside one of the windows to hold yourself still.

As you gaze out you see the shining jewel of the hotel grow gradually brighter. Now you can see it looks just like the picture in the VIP lounge back on Earth: a cylinder with several tubes along its sides and various other attachments. As it grows larger you see that it's covered with lights. These are the windows. They make the hotel look warm and inviting against the blackness of infinite space.

The Captain rotates the orbiter gently in preparation for docking and the Earth swings smoothly to one side of the window; the roof windows now face directly towards the hotel. The orbiter's docking port will be aligned with one of the entrances on the non-rotating body of the hotel and a flexible, airtight jetway is used to link the two. The Captain asks you to return to your seats and to fasten your seat belts in preparation for these manoeuvres.

There are a few slight jolts as Spacebus moves into position and grapples are secured. Crew members check the integrity of the airtight seals and signal to the cabin staff to go ahead and open the airlock. The Captain reminds you not to leave anything behind, then welcomes you to the space hotel and wishes you a pleasant stay.

Cabin staff help you unfasten your seat belt. You collect your belongings, Velcro them to your chest, and float towards the door. It's all rather like leaving a terrestrial airliner after a journey, except that on Earth you don't float into the arrivals hall. The jetway which connects the orbiter with the docking bay is lined with handholds, so moving forwards is not too difficult. You have to make an effort to overcome the temptation to let go and enjoy the total freedom of weightlessness.

You step out of the jetway into the hotel atrium, a large, circular room with corridors leading off in several directions. Since this part of the hotel is in zero gravity you hold on to one of the railings provided. The hotel manager and a group of staff come forward to welcome your party and to divide you into a number of groups, to each of which is assigned a member of staff. Yours explains that her first jobs are to remind you of the layout of the hotel and its facilities; and to take you to your rooms.

The space hotel is a huge structure 100 m (330 ft) in diameter and the largest spacecraft in orbit. With its lights blazing against the inky blackness of space it floats in orbit 500 km (300 mls) above the Earth. The outer structure, built of cylindrical aluminium sections, revolves approximately once every 40 seconds to create artificial gravity within; zerogee conditions prevail in the non-rotating central core. The hotel is assembled in orbit from smaller sections prefabricated on Earth and launched in cargo-carrying spacecraft.

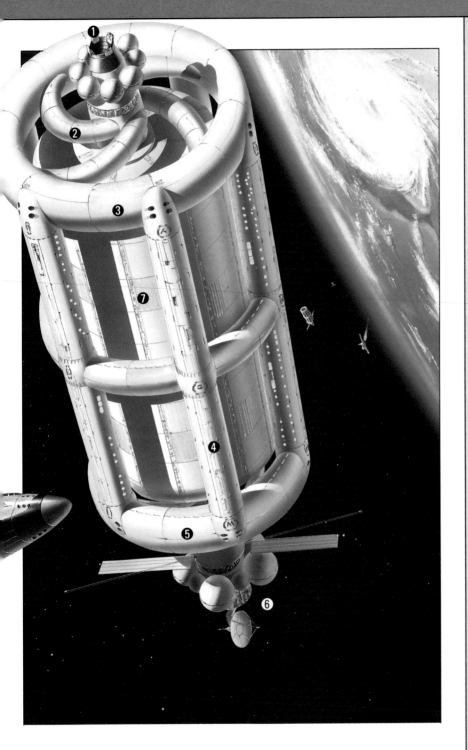

DOCKING AREA ❶
The orbiter docks with the central axis of the hotel (*left*). To make docking easier, the hotel docking area is 'de-spun' from the main part of the hotel – that is, it is not rotating. When it is in position (*below*), Spacebus is secured by grapples and connected to the hotel's central atrium by an airlock.

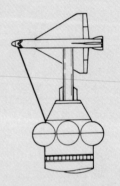

SLOPING STAIRWAYS ❷

NORTH RING ❸

ACCOMMODATION AREAS ❹

SOUTH RING ❺

OBSERVATION ROOMS ❻

ACTIVITY AREA ❼

The guide leads you across the hotel atrium to another, cylindrical, room leading off it, from which slope passages leading out from the centre – apparently up and down – but since there is no gravity 'up' and 'down' can be any direction. As you float into the room the guide helps you move to one side and you find yourself standing against its concave outer wall. Then you follow your guide along a passage which slopes down through the room's curved floor. As you move along the passage, walking gets easier. The artificial gravity increases as you move further away from the hub of what is really a large, slowly-rotating wheel.

By the time your weight reaches about 10 kilograms (22 pounds) the passage has opened into another, wider corridor, the hotel's North Ring. Your guide leads you right around it, showing how it forms a full circle. Dining rooms, lounges, bars and recreation rooms open off it on both sides, separated by the entrances to corridors leading south, which form the main accommodation area.

You turn south along your accommodation arm, confident that you're walking upright, although, your head is pointing towards the hotel's central axis. You come to where the South Ring joins the end of all the north-south corridors. This is the administration wing, where the staff offices are located. You're led around this and then up another sloping corridor to the lower part of the hotel's central hub. Connected to the south side of the hub are a number of observation rooms. These are de-spun, that is, they rotate gently in the opposite direction from the rest of the hotel to allow viewing in any direction and they are permanently darkened to provide perfect viewing conditions. They're in zero gravity, enabling guests to look through the windows in any orientation.

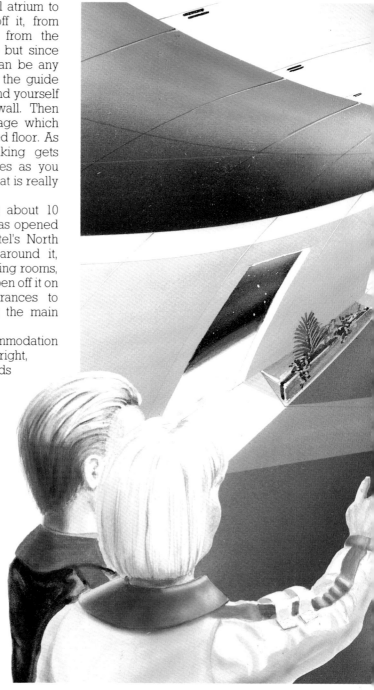

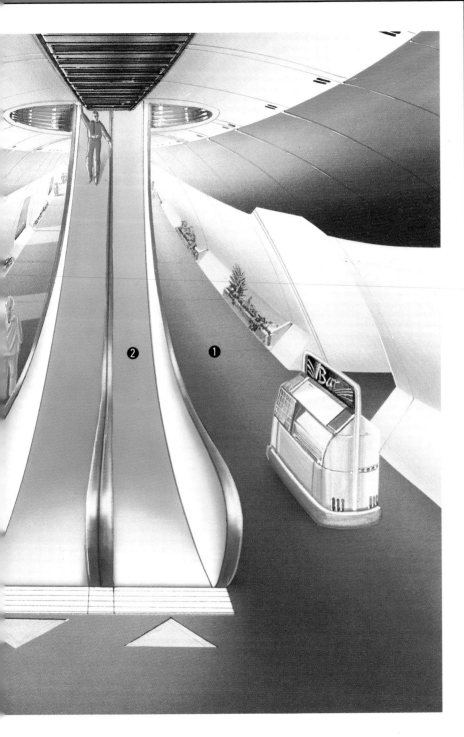

Many sloping passages (*left*) lead off the cylindrical rooms adjoining the hotel's atrium. There is no gravity in the hub of the hotel, and when you are floating, 'up' and 'down' can be any direction. The artificial gravity increases as you move further away from the hub of what is really a large, slowly-rotating wheel (**1**) – so your weight increases and walking gets easier. By the time you reach the North Ring at the end of the passage your weight is about one-sixth of your earthbound weight: 10 kg (22 lb). The South Ring of the hotel has similar passages (**2**) leading up to the south hub where the observation rooms are located.

LIVING IN ORBIT

This hotel is big and luxurious enough to have rooms of all sizes: single, double, twin and family. Your room is like any small hotel room in many respects, but it has two major differences: you weigh less in it and you look out of the windows into space. You find the view from your bedroom windows hypnotic. You gaze alternately at the Earth and the Sun, which fill the horizon almost twice per minute as the hotel turns on its axis; and out into the sparkling infinity of space. Off to one side you can see one of the other accommodation arms and at times you can see a space vehicle. The windows are fitted with photochromic glass, which responds to glare by darkening. The degree of shading afforded by the photochromic glass can be adjusted manually, so you can reduce the glare from the Sun if you find it annoying; and you can turn the sunlight right off when you want to sleep.

One of the major advantages of low-gravity living is that sleep is more comfortable than in the gravitational conditions on Earth. Because the parts of your body in contact with the mattress are less compressed, your body is less influenced by the shape of the mattress, so it takes up a more relaxed position. Changing position is also easier. And what could be more conducive to deep sleep than staring from your pillow at distant galaxies in deepest space?

Guests who share a bed find that low gravity has other advantages: for example, your arms and legs won't go to sleep if your partner lies on them. A bed cover attached by Velcro at the corners can help to keep you in bed, but if you are too lively the Velcro may peel back and you'll fly across the room. Exploring this and other novelties of weightlessness have added a dimension to the concept of the honeymoon, for which space hotels, with suites available in both partial and zero gravity, are finding an enthusiastic market. There are even entertaining books on sale giving helpful advice on such delicate but tricky matters as 'rendezvous and docking' in zero gravity.

Your guide drops in once or twice while you're settling in to make sure there are no problems and to answer questions. When you're all ready she comes back to lead your group down the corridor to a meeting room off the Centre Ring which, as its name suggests, encircles the centre of the hotel and opens on to more facilities. Here your party will be able to have a snack and to meet with the chief guide to discuss your timetable for the next few days. This room will serve as a common room for the use of your party at any time during your stay.

The kitchens of this new hotel have been staffed by some of the best chefs in the food business and they aim to cater for every diet and every taste. Generally, guests living in low gravity and spending part of their time in zero gravity prefer to eat several light snacks during the day, rather than one or two heavy meals, so the kitchen staff offer hot and cold snacks 24 hours a day.

Most of the guests prefer to use the cafés, bars, restaurants and lounges in the low-gravity sections in the centre of the hotel, where the catering and eating are much the same as on Earth. But some also like to try the unique experience of eating in zero gravity, like the pioneer astronauts last century. A canteen has therefore been built in the zero gravity part of the hotel. Velcro-covered seats keep you anchored to your place at the table and snap-together trays and dishes keep your food in place. Inevitably many guests (not just the children) can't resist playing tricks, like floating a blob of orange juice in mid air and drinking it through a straw, or sending a grape floating over to someone across the other side of the room.

More entertainment from zero-gravity conditions can be found in the demonstration rooms in the hotel's Centre Ring, where guests can watch objects behaving in strange and surprising ways under zero gravity. Demonstrators set objects of different shapes and sizes spinning in mid-air; make magnetic materials float under the influence of the Earth's magnetic field and other, artificial, fields;

On the north side of the hub is the main entrance to the zerogee activity area, where the hotel's most spectacular facilities, the space-sports halls, are located.

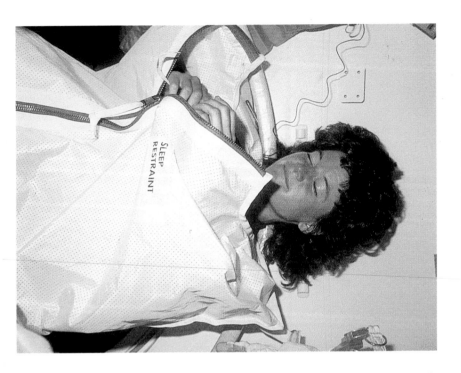

SLEEPING

To sleep in weightless conditions you need some sort of sleep restraint device to stop you floating around. In the photograph (*left*) astronaut Dr Sally Ride turns in on the 7th Space Shuttle flight (STS-7), way back in June 1983. Space hotel guests will not need to do this since artificial gravity prevails in the hotel's accommodation areas.

SHOWERING

To shower in zero gravity can be a bit like a game of chase the raindrops; on Earth it's gravity that keeps the rain falling downwards, an excellent system which will be reproduced artificially for the benefit of the guests in the space hotel. On Skylab back in 1974 (*left*) astronauts showered inside curtains pulled up from the floor and attached to the ceiling, forming a cylinder in which the water would be contained. The water did not fall, but floated about until it was drawn off by a suction system. The hotel also has showers in artificial gravity for those who want to get clean quickly.

85

SPACE-SPORTS

The space-sports complex consists of a number of de-spun rooms as large as the full width of the hotel, where guests can practise new sports in both zero and partial gravity.

Many guests, even those on their second visit, like to visit the gymn on their first day, to practise some of the gentle movements in zero gravity they learned during the last few days at the Centre back on Earth. Guided by an instructor, you try them out briefly and have little difficulty and lots of fun learning how to push off gently from a wall without tumbling; then how to push off with a slight offset so as to rotate and land on your feet on the opposite wall. You quickly get faster, add in more spins, and make a mental note to come back and try out a few more ideas later.

Once you have learned some of the basic skills, the range of gymnastic activities possible in low and zero gravity is as wide as your imagination. You can try out group gymnastics (similar to synchronized swimming); individual and team ball games, from basketball, football and tennis to new ones, invented to take advantage of the unique location. You can have extra fun by playing any of these games in partial gravity in one of the slowly-rotating chambers, where a thrown ball follows an extraordinary corkscrew trajectory.

FLYING

In the zero and partial gravity environments aboard the hotel you can fly like the early aviators tried to: wearing wings made from fabric stretched over a light framework. In the zero gravity of the hotel flying is easier than in gravity, since there's no need to keep your wings beating in order to remain airborne, but you need the help of an instructor to learn to use them correctly and (most importantly) to come to a halt.

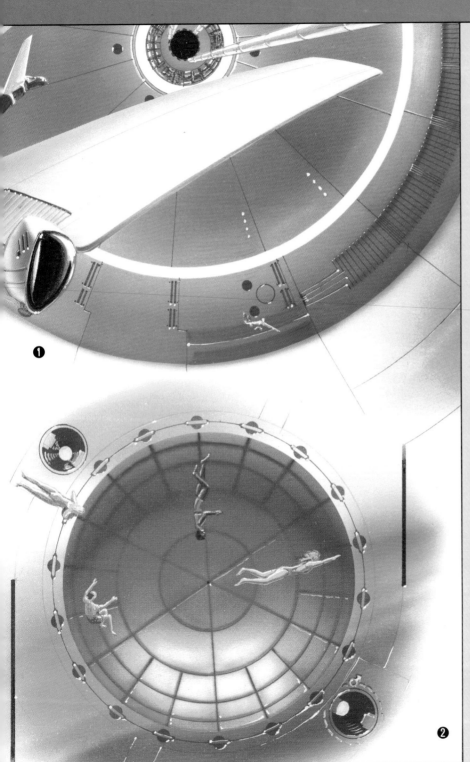

The unique leisure area is the subject of the space hotel's best-selling postcards. Newly-arrived guests flock to the gymnasium to explore their new-found freedom of movement. You start by getting the feel of pushing yourself off lightly with your feet and drifting very slowly around the room. Your body keeps moving smoothly in a straight line until you reach an obstacle. As you drift along you can move your body as you like, even turn round, while moving. As you become skilled at going where you want to you learn to set yourself somersaults.

Learn to fly like a bird in the space hotel's zero and partial gravity environments, wearing lightweight wings attached to your arms by a sleeve and a hand-grip; and a stabilizer, like the tailplane of an aircraft, attached to your feet. You'll need instruction in how to keep your balance while flapping your wings to bring yourself to a controlled stop. When you've mastered take-off, hovering and landing, you'll be taught to accelerate, turn and swoop.

The trampoline room is cylindrical with elastic sides which you can treat as a three-dimensional trampoline. In a weightless environment there is no fear of injury by falling on to a hard floor.

87

The hotel's swimming facilities are justifiably famous back on Earth. They are possible only in space. The main pool is inside an enormous Perspex-sided drum, which rotates gently to keep the water in place. Because there is no gravity along its axis, the water doesn't settle in the bottom half of the drum, but adheres to the sides like an inner lining, so that swimmers can describe a circle around the inside. You can swim on or beneath the inner surface of the drum (much as in a swimming pool on Earth), but you can do acrobatics in and out of the water, and you can dive out of the water into the air space above it. You can also detach armfuls of water and send them wobbling across the centre of the pool. Water will never be the same again, you decide, now that you have experienced this.

The zero-gravity water rooms are especially popular with children. You watch them and have to admit that you, too, want to play with blobs of water, throwing small ones like snowballs at other kids; using them to propel yourself forward by throwing them in the opposite direction; and playing chasing games. You can swim in larger blobs; make them into entertaining shapes by spinning them; or blow bubbles in them.

Like all the hotel's facilities, the water rooms are supervised by qualified staff, whose job is to ensure that the highest standards of safety are maintained – not only of equipment but also of the guests' behaviour. For example, in all the water rooms guests wear suspended around their necks small bottles of compressed air with a mouthpiece to enable them to breathe if they need to when immersed in water.

In the demonstration rooms, the staff demonstrate and explain the strange ways in which liquids seem to behave. Water, for example, tends to take up a spherical shape in zero gravity and if bubbles are blown into it they don't rise to the surface, because there's no up nor down. You can take part yourself, separating the bubbles from the liquid by setting it spinning, so that the bubbles move to the centre to form a single large bubble, which can be burst to leave a rotating doughnut-shaped ring of water.

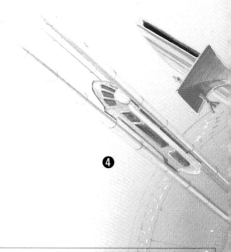

❹

WEIGHTLESSNESS

The weight of your body is due to the force of gravity acting upon you: the Earth's gravitational attraction pulling you towards its centre. What you feel as weight is the force on that part of you touching the ground or an extension of it, such as a chair. Remove the resistance to gravity by removing all the supports – by diving off a diving board, for instance – and you feel weightless, although the force of gravity and your weight are still there. Your body will then follow a free-fall trajectory. In the space hotel gravity is still acting on both you and the environment, but the hotel follows a free-fall trajectory, like your body in a dive. It describes a circular orbit, in which the curvature of the hotel's free-fall trajectory keeps it orbiting the Earth at a steady height. Inside the hotel there is no resistance to gravity, so no reaction to your weight, and you feel weightless, except in the accommodation areas, which are spun, that is, gently rotating to create artificial gravity. The rotation holds you against the outer walls, with a force of about one-sixth of your earthbound weight.

The swimming room (*left*) occupies the entire diameter of the space hotel's central core, where very gentle rotation keeps the water adhering to the curved sides (**1**). This enables you to swim in it or to take off like a flying fish and dive across it. In a low-g environment the water is lightweight, so you can detach blobs of it and toss them like balls to a partner swimming over the other side. The diving boards (**2**) are high – instead of diving you fly into the water. In another water room is a huge blob of water for children to play with; they might dive into it or pick it up and throw it against the room's curved sides, where it splashes into pieces, which float away in every direction. Above the water people practise flying (**3**), or take rides on the overhead monorail (**4**), which tours the hotel's leisure facilities.

89

EARTH-GAZING

One thing the hotel guests never tire of is watching the Earth passing silently beneath the hotel windows. At an altitude of a few hundred miles or kilometres you are still very near the Earth's surface by comparison with its size. It almost fills the field of view when you look through a window towards it. Many writers have tried to describe the feeling of seeing for the first time the Earth as a planet: a fragile and precious cradle for life among hundreds of light years of inanimate stars.

On each orbit of the Earth, which takes about an hour and a half, the hotel follows a different track over the ground, so the landmarks continually change. Some of the more dramatic sights to be seen by day are the marks of prehistoric impacts suffered by the Earth from collisions with asteroids (boulders, some the size of mountains, orbiting the Sun).

The dark side of the Earth is an equally fascinating and beautiful sight. Far from being pitch black, it is spangled with eerie lights. Lightning strikes the Earth approximately every one-hundredth of a second. Seen from above at night, this creates a fascinating sight, quite ghostly because it is silent. The aurorae near the Earth's magnetic poles are particularly dramatic. They can be seen from above as rippling cones of light, caused by charged particles from the Sun rushing down along the magnetic field-lines of the Earth and ionizing the atmospheric gases as they converge near the Pole. They come up almost to the space hotel, giving the impression that you're floating over a translucent ocean.

You may see such unusual sights as outbursts of phosphorescence in the oceans, or a volcano pouring out lava. Then there's the regular delight of seeing dusk and dawn outline the limb of the darkened Earth with beautiful multi-coloured bands of light.

Spectacular views of the Earth provide the ultimate thrill of a space holiday. The space hotel will be sufficiently near the Earth to enable visitors using the binoculars and telescopes in the observation lounges to spot easily-identifiable areas. On a cloudy day parts of the Earth's surface may be obscured, but on a clear day a feature such as the Hawaiian island chain (*right*) would be identifiable without telescopic aids through the hotel's large windows.

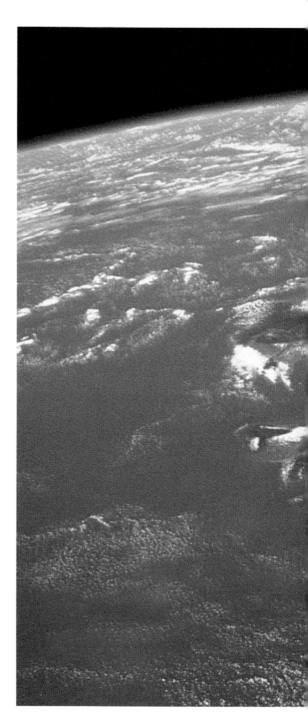

MOUNTAINS & DESERTS

Conquering the Earth's highest mountains has always been a challenge. Climbers reach the peaks on foot and the less intrepid can fly through mountains in an aeroplane as a way of sharing in this exhilarating experience. So far, only astronauts have been able to look down upon high peaks and mountain ranges from space; soon, space tourists will be able to share the experience. Glaciers are easily spotted and especially impressive from space. They shine out from the polar regions, as well as from high mountains – they form in those parts of the world where more snow falls than is lost through melting and evaporation. Splashes of blue in the mountains from rivers and lakes add colour to the view.

Deserts, almost as formidable as the Earth's highest peaks, may be easier to identify than mountains because they cover a vast area of the Earth's surface. They vary dramatically in colour, from vivid reds and yellows to dark grey. Rippling patterns in the sand caused by the wind make interesting viewing from above.

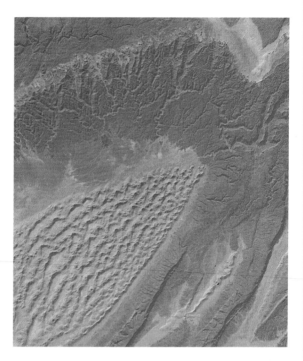

The Swiss Alps cradle Lake Geneva near the top of the photograph (*left*). The River Rhône, which feeds Lake Geneva, passes through a deep glaciated valley running down towards the right. From above, you appreciate the awesome scale of the Earth's most daunting peaks such as Mount McKinley (*far left*), the highest peak in North America, and the greatest ranges, such as the Himalayas (*below left*). You may be too far up, however, to spot the Yeti.

This image of the Namibian Desert (*below*) shows a large, circular formation, 2,580 m (8,500 ft) in height, called the Brandberg configuration. The position of Algeria's undulating Tifernine Dunes, standing 1,000 m (3,300 ft) high, trapped in the Tossili Najjar Mountains, is clear from the elevated angle of space (*right*).

OCEANS & RIVERS

The gentle blue of the oceans gives the planet Earth a luminescent beauty. About 70 per cent of its surface is covered with water. Seen from space the oceans look rounded, even mountainous, not flat as they do on Earth. Ocean currents and underwater mountains and valleys account for the variations in depth and height.

Lakes, rivers, ice floes and glaciers are as visible from orbit as oceans and seas. With guidance, the most amateur of geographers soon learns to pinpoint famous and familiar stretches of water: Lake Victoria, for example, the Nile or Antarctica. Videos and lectures on geography are a popular form of entertainment for tourists in the orbiting space hotel.

Being able to observe the Earth from space could make geography the most popular subject in any college curriculum if space trips were to be added to the range of compulsory field trips. Some space hotels might specialize in parties of students and professionals keen to study meteorology, oceanography, glaciation or perhaps land-formation from the vantage point of space. Observation lounges of space hotels might become venues for lectures conducted with an emphasis placed firmly on looking out of the windows, a practice not normally encouraged by teachers or lecturers.

It is not difficult to work out why the Colorado River Delta (*below left*) is nicknamed the 'burning tree'. Lake Nasser and the Aswan Dam (*right*) make an equally impressive view from space. The Aswan Dam is the barrier near the top of the picture, separating the lighter waters of the lake from the dark blue of the River Nile. To the trained eye it is obvious there has been a drought in this region of north-central Africa, the evidence being the exposed areas of lakebed, notably in the lower left corner of the photograph.

Clearly visible from space is the aptly-named Tongue of the Ocean (*below*), the deep blue, tongue-shaped area curling down from the top of the photograph. The Tongue is a great valley of water, over 1,000 m (3,000 ft) deep, surrounded by the shallow waters of the Great Bahama Bank.

WEATHER & CLOUD PATTERNS

When clouds – clusters of suspended water droplets – obscure your view of parts of the Earth's surface you may discover that they're interesting in their own right. Through their infinite variety of form clouds reveal global weather patterns. In the space hotel's observation rooms regular lectures, demonstrations, videos and computers are available for guests interested in learning to understand, record, interpret and even forecast the weather from the signs visible from space.

Freak weather makes especially interesting viewing from space. In the middle of the large photograph (*below centre*) Hurricane Juan (1985) can be seen clearly, having hit land and moved out into the Gulf of Mexico. Storms are the warning carried in the cloud formation above Zaïre (*bottom left*). Giant cumulonimbus clouds can measure up to 10 mls (16 km) in depth. Orderly chequered, roll-shaped or rounded formations are characteristic of the low-altitude stratocumulus, shown above the Pacific Ocean (*top left*). The change from tight clustering (on the left-hand side) to loose (on the right) may mark the edge of a cold current or an upwelling of warm water from the ocean depths.

A severe storm in the Bering Sea shows the Kamchatka Peninsula (*below*) hiding behind the cloud on the left. Cirrus clouds, which look as if they are made up of strands of hair or wool, were photographed over the Atlantic, 160 km (100 mls) north-west of Dakar, Africa (*bottom*). The clouds probably mark the location of a strong subtropical jetstream; the transverse bands may indicate a spiralling circulation within the jetstream. Meteorology aside, clouds make the Earth look beautiful from space, swathing the blue in soft white.

THE MOON

The Moon looks much clearer from space, where there is no atmosphere to distort its image or obscure the view as there is on Earth. However, as the Moon is a quarter of a million miles from the Earth and the space hotel is only 200 to 300 miles (500 to 600 kilometres) up, the Moon will not look much nearer than it does from Earth, but its pitted surface will hold the same fascination, especially through the telescopes and other instruments available in the hotel. Maps of the Moon's surface help you identify the craters – large, circular depressions formed when asteroids collide with the Moon; and the seas – large, flat plains created by the spread of molten lava from volcanic activity on the Moon.

In this close-up of the early crescent Moon (*below*) you can glimpse the Mare Crisium, the 'Sea of Crises', the irregular dark region just above the centre right of the photograph.

This oblique view of the far side of the Moon (*above*) shows a large central crater with a diameter of 80 km (50 mls).

The Moon's seas and craters have fanciful names. The dark circular sea in the upper left area of this photograph (*left*) is the Mare Crisium, the 'Sea of Crises'. The irregular dark region just above and to the left of it is the Mare Tranquillitatis, the 'Sea of Tranquility' and below it is the Mare Fecunditatis, the 'Sea of Fertility'. At the Moon's bottom right edge is a conspicuous dark crater with a bright central peak. This was christened Tsiolkovsky, after the famous Russian inventor of rockets.

Stars look much brighter from space than from Earth, but they do not twinkle, because twinkling is an effect caused by the atmosphere. From space their colours are much more distinct. Some stars are vivid red, blues and greens. From the space hotel the constellations look the same however; the stars are so far away that you would have to travel very far indeed for the constellations to change in appearance.

In the southern sky is Antares (Alpha Scorpionis) (*right*), a bright, reddish star. It is a conspicuous red supergiant, the brightest star in the constellation of Scorpius. The bright object to the right of Antares is a globular star cluster. Also in the northern sky can be seen this region of interacting or merging galaxies, 60 million light years away, known as the Antennae (*below left*).

In the northern sky is the Perseus region of the Milky Way (*far right*). The two red, hazy objects at the top of the image are star clusters surrounded by clouds of fluorescent hydrogen gas. The centre of our galaxy, which is called the Milky Way, is the subject of the photograph *below right*. The tracks were left by a passing man-made satellite.

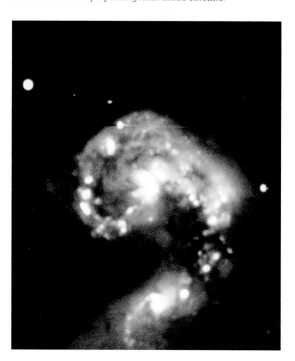

Knowing the flight home will be an experience to savour makes the end of your holiday a little less sorrowful than it might be. On your last morning you go out to watch the upcoming Spacebus arrive, carrying new guests. You, now an expert, watch their first zero-g fumbles with benign amusement. You collect your bag and make your way to the departure lounge, in the zero-gravity hub of the North Ring.

The hotel manager wishes you goodbye and you pass expertly along the jetway connecting with the orbiter, and take your seat aboard. The Captain welcomes everyone aboard and the doors are shut in preparation for de-orbiting.

You feel a slight jolt as the orbiter is pushed away from the space hotel by pneumatic pistons. For about 30 seconds, as the engines thrust, you feel a surge of weight in your back. Then it is back to zero-g for about 20 minutes as the craft drifts towards the atmosphere. The orbiter falls faster and faster and the thin air around it heats up and starts to glow as it streams past the windows. The upward pressure of the air on the orbiter's belly presses you into your seat and for a short while you feel nearly one and a half times your normal earthbound weight.

The blackness of space lightens to deep blue, then to the brilliant blue sky of the upper atmosphere. As the clouds come nearer you hear the rush of air outside the cabin.

Travelling south east over the North Atlantic, the Captain rolls the orbiter gently from side to side so you can see over the big wings. The English Channel is below and northern France to your right. She starts up the landing-jets, signalling the beginning of the long turn to port to head the craft towards the runway of the Bristol Aerospaceport. After the novelty of re-entry, coming in on final approach seems too much like the end of an ordinary airline flight.

After touch-down you make your way to the terminal, wondering how long it will be before you can visit space again. But space holidays are now so popular that Orbitours are expanding the possibilities: they're offering discount schemes and professionally-managed savings plans to make it easier for you to holiday above the sky.

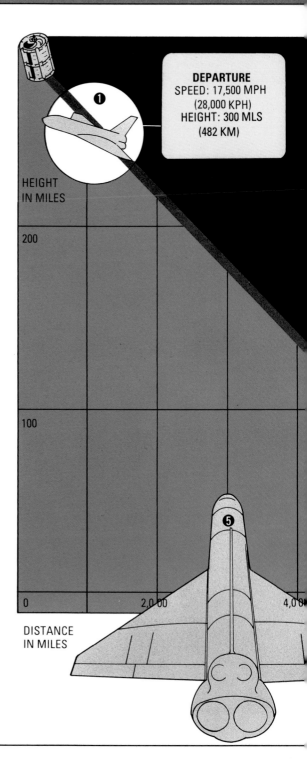

DEPARTURE
SPEED: 17,500 MPH
(28,000 KPH)
HEIGHT: 300 MLS
(482 KM)

HEIGHT
IN MILES

200

100

0

DISTANCE
IN MILES

2,000

4,000

Although there is no impression of speed, the hotel is travelling at 17,500 mph (28,000 kph). To break away, the orbiter must reduce speed well below that of the hotel, so that it falls back into the atmosphere, entering the atmosphere at a speed of 16,700 mph (27,000 kph), causing the air around it to heat up with friction. The heat ionizes the air around the orbiter, so that radio waves cannot pass through. Since the orbiter glides into the atmosphere there is no engine noise as there would be in an airliner, until, at 20,000 ft (6 km) the landing jets are started up for the turn into the approach to the aerospaceport.

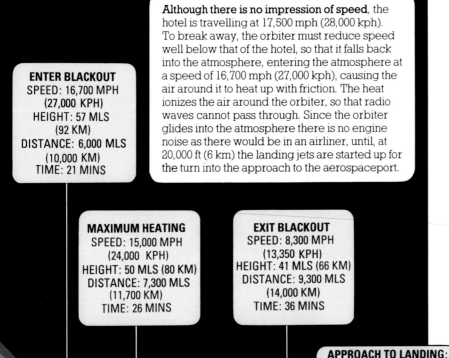

ENTER BLACKOUT
SPEED: 16,700 MPH
(27,000 KPH)
HEIGHT: 57 MLS
(92 KM)
DISTANCE: 6,000 MLS
(10,000 KM)
TIME: 21 MINS

MAXIMUM HEATING
SPEED: 15,000 MPH
(24,000 KPH)
HEIGHT: 50 MLS (80 KM)
DISTANCE: 7,300 MLS
(11,700 KM)
TIME: 26 MINS

EXIT BLACKOUT
SPEED: 8,300 MPH
(13,350 KPH)
HEIGHT: 41 MLS (66 KM)
DISTANCE: 9,300 MLS
(14,000 KM)
TIME: 36 MINS

APPROACH TO LANDING:
SPEED: SUBSONIC
(600 MPH/1,000 KPH)
HEIGHT: 8 MLS (13 KM)
DISTANCE: 10,000 MLS
(16,000 KM)
TIME: 46 MINS

6,000   8,000   10,000

 ①

The orbiter starts its return journey by pointing backwards along the flight path and firing the rocket motors to slow it down.

 ②

The Captain keeps the nose high so that the craft meets the air belly first to slow it down most effectively. Aerodynamic heating results in a radio blackout.

 ③

The orbiter reaches the atmosphere at a height of about 57 mls (92 km). Aerodynamic heating reaches its maximum intensity.

 ④

Aerodynamic heating is reduced and radio contact resumes. The orbiter glides down into the lower atmosphere, its speed falling to subsonic.

⑤

On the approach to the runway beams from the aerospaceport's microwave landing system lock on to the orbiter's landing guidance system, commanding the electronic controls to operate them automatically and fly the craft towards the runway. The Captain monitors the automatic operation until, a few minutes before landing, she takes over control.

6 THE COSTS AND BENEFITS

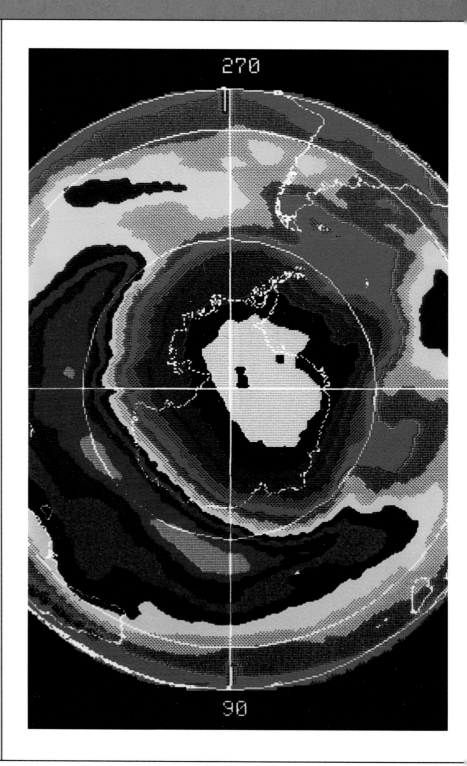

A Catch 22 situation reduces the probability that ordinary people will have the chance to travel into space in the near future: the development of tourism in space depends upon operators being able to achieve low space transportation costs, but these cannot be achieved without correspondingly high traffic levels. Yet, as Chapter 1 demonstrates, the market is ready for space tourism. As well as the Gallup Poll survey for American Express (see page 9), other informal surveys indicate strongly that large numbers of people want to visit space. Moreover, there is little doubt that a trip into space would be the experience of a lifetime, as Chapter 5 shows. Worldwide reports of the first passengers' experiences would assuredly lead to an escalation of demand.

Chapter 2 traces why, more than 20 years after the first person landed on the Moon, only trained astronauts are allowed to go into space. It also accounts for the persistence of that extraordinarily costly phenomenon, the launch vehicle that can be used only once. And it explains how a cost-effective alternative could already be carrying holidaymakers into orbit.

As well as the market, the technology is ready for space tourism. The few unsolved technical problems are explained in Chapter 3, in which we also illustrate and describe Spacecab, a small spaceplane, which could be built now, using technology that has already been developed. Finally, Chapter 4 shows that there are no insurmountable safety problems.

What, then, are the chances of space tourism being developed soon? The present plans are

The unique view of Earth from space is already being exploited by weather and earth-viewing satellites. Their use has improved scientists' understanding of geology, land use, water distribution, oceanography and pollution. Sensitive instruments can measure the distribution of air pollution on a global scale, making the measurement of pollution on Earth particularly effective when carried out from space. For example, the thinning of the ozone layer can be seen clearly in the photograph (left) of ozone over Antarctica. The extent of the destruction of rain forests and even the growing of illegal drugs can be detected by orbiting instruments. The photographs they transmit can be used as direct evidence of their activities to industrial culprits.

not encouraging. Visits by the public are not on the list of proposed uses of Freedom, the planned NASA/International Space Station (see page 15); and existing launch vehicles are not suitable for early space tourism. There is, however, more than one spaceplane currently at the planning stage.

ON THE DRAWING BOARD

The U.S. National Aerospace Plane (NASP) is a proposed single-stage-to-orbit vehicle. A demonstrator/prototype, the X-30, is scheduled to fly in the late nineteen-nineties. An operational version could be available around 2010, but it would need several years of operation before being suitable to carry passengers. Moreover, as a single-stage vehicle it requires more advanced technology than would a two-stage vehicle like Spacebus.

However, it need not be a priority to develop single-stage operation as early as this. Since Spacebus is expected to achieve lower costs than the Space Shuttle by a factor of 1,000 on a direct cost per seat basis during the second, exclusive stage of space travel development (see page 10), reusability is more urgent.

Hermes (see page 107) is a proposed European piloted spacecraft being designed as we write; its full development for a first piloted flight in 1999 is to be decided on soon. It will be launched on the Ariane 5 expendable launch vehicle, now under development as a successor to Ariane 4, intended primarily for the launching of large communications satellites. It perpetuates the cost and safety problems of vehicles with expendable stages (see below **The cost of safety**), so it is unsuitable for space tourism. It is similar to the Boeing X-20 Dyna Soar (see page 27), cancelled in 1963. Thus, Hermes is 20 years late and NASP is 20 years early.

Two-stage launchers which could be used for tourism are being studied, but there are no firm plans to develop them. Among them are the German MBB Sänger project and the US Space Van. Sänger is not unlike Spacebus, but it lacks the design features necessary for early develop-

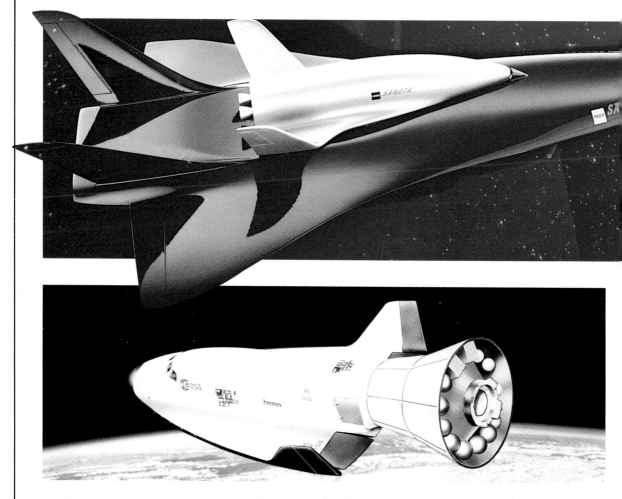

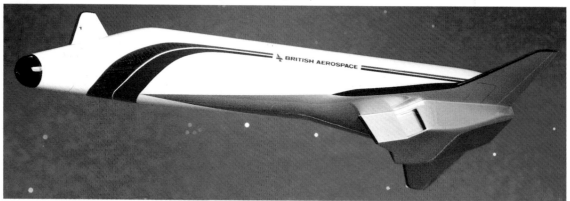

ment. For example, the booster has jet engines only, which have to be extremely advanced to achieve the required separation speed of Mach 7; Spacebus uses off-the-shelf rocket engines for the difficult high-speed part of the boost phase. The Sänger project lacks the ski-jump separation of Spacebus (*see page 48*), so the orbiter has to fly out of the atmosphere using atmospheric lift, exposed to high air loads and to severe aerodynamic heating. The Spacebus orbiter avoids exposure to both on the way up. Nonetheless, of all the current official projects, Sänger is most suitable for tourism. Indeed, MBB have proposed a passenger-carrying version with 36 seats, which could be in service by 2015.

Looking further into the future, NASA, ESA and Japan are considering a lunar base followed by

Sänger (*top left*) is an MBB proposal for a two-stage spaceplane which is being partly funded by the West German government. It is similar in several basic respects to Spacebus, but uses all-new engines and lacks other features aimed at reducing development costs.

Hermes (*centre left*) is an ESA proposal for a small piloted spacecraft to be launched by the expendable Ariane 5. It is basically a smaller version of the Space Shuttle and, if built, will suffer similar cost problems.

Hotol (*bottom left*) is a British Aerospace proposal for an unpiloted single-stage-to-orbit satellite launch vehicle. As it is designed for cargo-carrying, it is aimed at a different market from Spacecab and Spacebus, whose main purpose is transporting people.

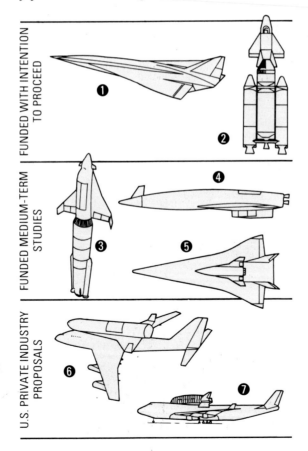

FUNDED WITH INTENTION TO PROCEED

FUNDED MEDIUM-TERM STUDIES

U.S. PRIVATE INDUSTRY PROPOSALS

Vehicles under consideration as we go to press are illustrated (*left*). The two receiving the most funding are the single-stage National Aerospace Plane (NASP) and Hermes. We think the NASP is some 20 years ahead of its time because two-stage vehicles can achieve costs about 1,000 times less than the Space Shuttle. Single-stagers are far more difficult technically and may one day reduce costs by a further factor of two. Also being funded are the Japanese Hope unpiloted research project, Hotol and Sänger. Two interesting US private industry proposals are the Teledyne Brown project and Space Van, but neither of these is funded as we write.

National Aerospace Plane ❶

Hermes ❷

Hope ❸

Hotol ❹

Sänger ❺

Teledyne Brown ❻

Space Van ❼

107

The EAP (Experimental Aircraft Programme, *below*) is a technology demonstrator for the forthcoming EFA (European Fighter Aircraft). One prototype has been built by British Aerospace at a cost of some $400 million (£240 million), less than 10% of the total development cost of EFA. It has made over 200 flights in four years. Hermes, of roughly similar size and shape, has an estimated development cost some 10 times greater, yet is planned to make only 40 flights over 10 years. We believe that the high costs and poor safety record of expendable launch vehicles are responsible for the high development cost and few flights of Hermes.

GEMINI

a trip to Mars for a small number of astronauts around 2020, at a cost of some $400 thousand million (£250 thousand million) – four times more than the costly nineteen-sixties' lunar visits.

Thus, progress towards reducing the cost of space travel is not being made as rapidly as might be possible with a more commercial approach, such as the development of tourism, which could result in a million passengers per year in about 20 years. Yet there are no official plans to so much as study space tourism, and the

The development cost trend lines in the graph (*centre right*) show that building a prototype aeroplane incurs some 10% of the total cost of developing a fully-operational version. Piloted spacecraft have cost about ten times more than prototype aeroplanes. We think that a factor of two is due to more difficult technology and a factor of five due to the safety problems resulting from the use of expendable launch vehicles. Spaceplanes are fully reusable and only the factor of two should apply. Thus a prototype of Spacecab should cost roughly twice that of the Concorde prototype and EAP combined (these have roughly the same weight as the booster and orbiter respectively). This totals about $2,000 million (£1,200 million) or about half the cost of Hermes.

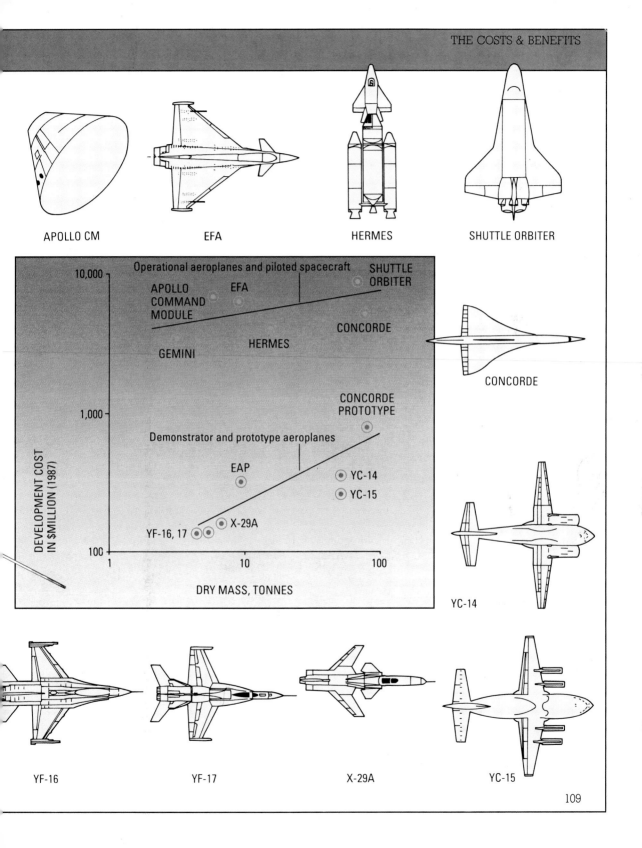

APOLLO CM

EFA

HERMES

SHUTTLE ORBITER

CONCORDE

YC-14

YF-16

YF-17

X-29A

YC-15

Operational aeroplanes and piloted spacecraft

SHUTTLE ORBITER

APOLLO COMMAND MODULE

EFA

CONCORDE

HERMES

GEMINI

10,000

1,000

CONCORDE PROTOTYPE

Demonstrator and prototype aeroplanes

EAP

YC-14

YC-15

YF-16, 17

X-29A

100

DEVELOPMENT COST IN $MILLION (1987)

DRY MASS, TONNES

1

10

100

realization of present plans would result in perhaps 100 astronauts per year by then, all paid for by the taxpayer.

DEVELOPING A SPACELINER

It is interesting to compare Spacecab's development costs with those of Hermes (*see above*), its closest rival in terms of size. Europe's desire to send people into orbit is the impetus behind Hermes. A small piloted spaceplane launched by a vehicle already in production is claimed to be the cheapest way to achieve the object, since only one new vehicle will be required. A fully-reusable spaceplane with two new stages and more advanced technology would cost more to develop, the logic goes. The argument seems plausible enough, but we would argue that Spacecab could be developed at a lower cost than Hermes. This conclusion is supported by the trend lines in the graph on page 109.

Hermes is roughly the same size as the Experimental Aircraft Programme (EAP, *see page 108*), a flying technology demonstrator/prototype for the forthcoming European Fighter Aircraft, and both vehicles use very advanced technology, so it might be expected that their development costs would be similar. Not so. The EAP cost about $400 million (£250 million) and the estimated development cost of Hermes at 1987 prices is ten times greater at $4 thousand million (£2.5 thousand million). Why this big difference? Hermes requires additional systems for operating in space, and a thermal protection system, but these should at most double the cost. That still leaves a factor of five to explain.

THE COST OF SAFETY

The answer we propose is that the extra cost is due to extra safety measures introduced to protect astronauts. Hermes uses expendable lower stages, which are considerably less safe than aeroplanes: they crash on average once every 50 flights compared with an airliner rate of one fatal crash per 1,000,000 flights. The risk is exacerbated by the very high cost of expend-

able launchers, which means that only a tiny number of test flights is carried out.

An experimental aeroplane takes, typically, 100 flights to reach the limits of its flight envelope and an airliner requires about 1,000 flights before it will be cleared for carrying passengers. An aeroplane flight test programme is planned to be progressive. Each flight is a little higher or faster than the one before, or tries out a new system or a new manoeuvre. The new (hence risky) aspects of each flight are carefully controlled and the total risk is spread over 100 or more flights. By contrast the Space Shuttle made six subsonic gliding flights before being hurtled into orbit. The cost per flight was too high to afford a gradual build-up, so many items crucial to safety had to work right first time.

The same factors of cost vs safety apply to any piloted spacecraft launched on an expendable vehicle. Mercury, Gemini and Apollo reached orbit with astronauts on board after a handful of flights; the same is planned for Hermes. Vast sums of money were therefore spent on providing escape rockets (the Space Shuttle was an exception), and on achieving high-quality production, ground-testing, reliability analysis and astronaut-training for adequate safety.

We suggest that this search for safety using expendable launchers has been the driving factor behind the high development cost of piloted spacecraft, and explains why it has cost so much more to qualify a piece of equipment for use on a piloted spacecraft than on an aeroplane. Given this flaw in the concept of transporting people on expendable launchers, the safety levels reached by the American and Soviet piloted spaceflight programmes have been a remarkable achievement.

Safety is an Achilles heel to present plans for space development. The key to the official way ahead is the Freedom Space Station (*see page 15*). The crew of eight will be ferried to and from Earth in the Space Shuttle. However, the Shuttle's fatal accident rate is currently estimated to be as high as two per cent. With the number of flights that will be necessary to supply Freedom, the chances of fatal accidents are unacceptably high, as the U.S. Congress's Office of Technology Assessment has admitted. Thus, plans to spend some $20 thousand million (£12.5 thousand million) on the Freedom Space Station, followed by 20 times as much again on returning to the Moon and travelling to Mars, are founded on an unsafe vehicle and no firm plans for a replacement. For present plans to succeed there is an urgent need for a safe crew transporter to space stations.

The prototype of a new aeroplane costs, typically, between five and ten per cent of the total cost of the fully-operational version, which must be thoroughly tested before it can be released for service. However, expendable launchers are so unsafe and expensive that a spaceliner would be safer and cheaper when developed only as far as prototype standard. Because spaceplanes, being fully reusable, avoid the safety cost penalty of expendable launchers, a prototype spaceplane should cost about twice as much (to allow for more difficult technology) as a prototype advanced aeroplane of comparable weight. A prototype of the Spacecab orbiter should therefore cost about $800 million (£500 million), or twice as much as the EAP (allowing for extra systems and thermal protection). Similarly, a prototype of Spacecab's booster should cost no more than twice as much as an advanced aeroplane of comparable size, such as the Concorde prototype, at about $1.2 thousand million (£750 million). The Spacecab prototype should cost some $2 thousand million (£1.2 thousand million), about 50 per cent of the estimated development cost of Hermes.

The prototype of Spacecab could enter service carrying professional astronauts after perhaps only 100 flights. It would still be flown by test pilots with extensive ground-control back-up; and it would need extensive maintenance between flights. Nevertheless, it should be a vast improvement on the Space Shuttle in terms of safety. The costs would fall as operators gained experience and as pre-production and production models required less maintenance. As costs fell it would be used more often, causing further cost reductions and so on until

mature aeroplane-like operations could be achieved. The existence of a prototype space-liner would trigger off this beneficial cost spiral and this key first step could be made for about $2 thousand million (£1.2 thousand million).

DEVELOPING A SPACE HOTEL

The establishment of our Spacecab/Spacebus proposal as a key first step towards space tourism would therefore greatly help the operation of the proposed space stations by providing safe transportation for their crews. However, space stations are still very expensive. The forthcoming NASA Freedom space station will cost some $20 thousand million (£12.5 thousand million), due to the very high cost of launching it and of sending up construction and repair crews. Once space transportation costs fall, the costs of space stations can be reduced. It is reasonable to assume that eventually space station or space hotel costs could be broadly comparable to those of airliners of similar size. Thus a space station with the internal capacity of a Boeing 747 should cost about the same: $100 million (£60 million) at 1987 prices. The saving in the cost of the wings, tail, engines and landing gear, which are not needed, should roughly balance the cost of solar power panels and of more complicated systems for controlling temperature, air supply, water and waste. The hotel could accommodate roughly one-tenth the number of tourists as the 747, perhaps about 40. Its cost of about $100 million (£60 million) is a fraction of the $20 thousand million (£12.5 thousand million) of the eight-person Freedom.

REDUCING RUNNING COSTS

Clearly, low operating costs (see page 49) are essential to eliminate the catch outlined in the first paragraph of this chapter. Generating high traffic levels depends on low transportation costs for space station crews; and on affordable fares for passengers. But how quickly could operating costs come down from the $4 million (£2.4 million) for the Space Shuttle (assuming a

70-passenger variant) to our suggested goal of $10,000 (£6,000)? Given an immediate start, the whole process could take as few as 20 years (see page 56). Chapter 3 indicates that a small spaceplane such as Spacecab could be developed, using existing technology, to meet exactly the requirement for a reusable launch vehicle with the capacity of a business jet; and that it could be followed by an enlarged version, Spacebus, which would achieve the goal fare level for a brief visit to space possibly as soon as 17 years from now. Spacecab, being fully reusable, avoids the safety penalties of expendable launchers.

FUNDING, THE MISSING LINK

Apart from the $2 thousand million (£1.2 thousand million) needed to develop the prototype Spacecab we have not estimated any subsequent development costs; further study is needed to come up with realistic estimates. However, Spacebus is likely to cost broadly the same as Sänger, which has been quoted at about $10 thousand million (£6.2 thousand million). A simple early space station using the Space Shuttle External Tank as its structure (see page 57) is being planned by the American company, External Tanks Co., for a few hundred million dollars. Thus for less than the planned $20 thousand million (£12.5 thousand million) cost of the Freedom Space Station, a medium-sized spaceliner and several simple space stations could be built.

As Chapter 2 explains there has been very little private funding for launch vehicle development, which has been driven by government agencies interested principally in defence and national prestige. This largely explains the failure to develop flyback boosters and spaceplanes (see pages 30-31) at the time when they first became feasible. The high costs that resulted from these policies have prevented the private sector from understanding that costs lower than one per cent of current launch costs could readily be achieved with reusable launch vehicles. Consequently, potentially large-scale

uses of launch vehicles, such as passenger transport, have not been seriously investigated. Moreover, the commercial uses of space so far have simply not been significant enough to change the direction of development away from its government-dominated pattern.

That leaves one more important question unanswered: where is the money to develop space tourism going to come from? Clearly, the size of the task calls for international collaboration. The sums of money and risks involved mean that large-scale private-sector funding is unlikely to be forthcoming at this stage; yet large amounts of taxpayers' money cannot be spent on developing luxury entertainment for the few. We propose a step-by-step evolution.

THE WAY AHEAD

The starting point is for a detailed study to be made of space tourism: the market, the technology needed, safety considerations, and the types of spaceplane and space station required. This study would investigate thoroughly all the assumptions and assertions made in this book. The result would be an authoritative feasibility report. A second, parallel, study should be made of the quickest and most cost-effective way of providing safe transport to space stations. We suspect that the answer would be a spaceplane very like Spacecab.

Assuming that the claims made in this book are more or less substantiated, the next step would be for government agencies to fund the development of a small spaceplane with the main short-term objective of providing safe and economical transportation for crews to and from space stations. Taxpayer funding of the roughly $2 thousand million (£1.2 thousand million) cost would be justified because fully-reusable launch vehicles would make the space stations more cost-effective.

Once in regular operation, the spaceplanes would rapidly become cheaper to operate, and flying to and from space stations would become like an airline operation. At this stage tourism entrepreneurs could contribute funding for the

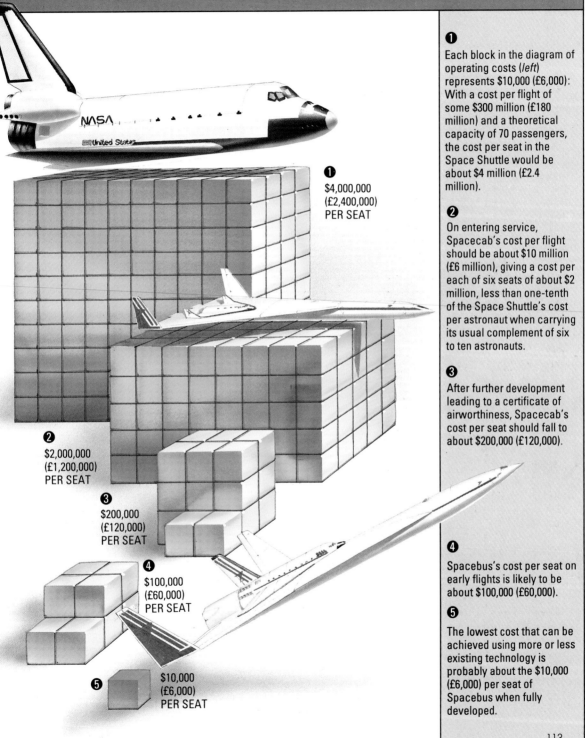

❶ $4,000,000 (£2,400,000) PER SEAT

❷ $2,000,000 (£1,200,000) PER SEAT

❸ $200,000 (£120,000) PER SEAT

❹ $100,000 (£60,000) PER SEAT

❺ $10,000 (£6,000) PER SEAT

❶
Each block in the diagram of operating costs (*left*) represents $10,000 (£6,000): With a cost per flight of some $300 million (£180 million) and a theoretical capacity of 70 passengers, the cost per seat in the Space Shuttle would be about $4 million (£2.4 million).

❷
On entering service, Spacecab's cost per flight should be about $10 million (£6 million), giving a cost per each of six seats of about $2 million, less than one-tenth of the Space Shuttle's cost per astronaut when carrying its usual complement of six to ten astronauts.

❸
After further development leading to a certificate of airworthiness, Spacecab's cost per seat should fall to about $200,000 (£120,000).

❹
Spacebus's cost per seat on early flights is likely to be about $100,000 (£60,000).

❺
The lowest cost that can be achieved using more or less existing technology is probably about the $10,000 (£6,000) per seat of Spacebus when fully developed.

113

additional safety-testing of the spaceplanes needed for passenger use. Thereafter the development of space tourism would be much like any other industry, with competition between companies and expansion using money raised in the marketplace. The prospect of $10 thousand million (£6.2 thousand million) in annual tourist revenues would justify multi-billion dollar investment. With the benefits of this low-cost infrastructure, returning to the Moon and visiting Mars would be far less expensive.

THE BENEFITS

If it develops as we suggest, tourism will become the most important commercial use of space and it will provide the funding for the development of lower-cost space-going vehicles and space stations. By driving space transportation costs down towards the levels of the aviation industry, it will provide much easier access to space for scientific and commercial, as well as governmental, uses.

In the field of astronomy, for example, everyday access to space opens up the possibility of crewed observatories carrying larger and more powerful instruments than are now possible, such as radio telescopes thousands of miles long and optical telescopes tens of metres in diameter. It will be economical for probes to land on most planets in the solar system and bring back samples, which will improve understanding of the formation of the solar system and the origins of life.

A major international programme is under way to understand the complex energy and chemical balance of land, sea and air. The aim of this programme, called Mission to Earth, is to increase understanding of the impact of the human race on the Earth and bring about more sensible control. The availability of spaceplanes to service the new satellites in orbit would greatly ease the project's design problems and reduce its operating costs.

The energy reaching the Earth from the Sun is 10,000 times that generated by human power systems. Huge solar power satellites have been proposed which would collect solar energy with arrays of solar cells covering hundreds of square kilometres, convert it into electricity and beam it to Earth as microwaves. Much of our energy needs could be met by this method, with minimal pollution on Earth, although major problems remain to be solved. High transportation costs have so far prevented even small pilot schemes, but this barrier would be removed as a result of the lower costs following from space tourism.

From a commercial point of view the weightless conditions in space have made possible significant experiments in materials science, crystal formation and many other fields. Reducing transportation costs will remove a barrier to progress, thus enabling products such as highly pure drugs and crystals for microprocessors to be manufactured in space. Jewellery made in zero gravity could have startling new designs.

Space travel will not be a panacea for all the ills of the modern world, but it should help to make the Earth a better place. Many of the astronauts who have been privileged to visit space have declared that their perspective of the Earth and the universe changed as a result of the experience. They became more concerned for the safety of the planet than with national advantage. When millions of people visit space it is very likely that the way the peoples of the Earth view their planet will change for the better.

GLOSSARY

Aerodynamics
The study of the forces exerted by a gas on a moving object.

Aerodynamic heating
This occurs when a vehicle re-entering the atmosphere is flying so fast that the friction from the air causes intense heating.

Aerospace transporter
A term in common currency in the nineteen-seventies meaning 'spaceplane' (q.v.).

Air-breathing engine
A jet engine (q.v.).

Air loads
The pressure on the skin of an aircraft from the airstream.

Airlock
An airtight passage between two pressurized vehicles, or sections within a vehicle.

Aurorae
Stream-like luminosity in the atmosphere, usually yellow, green or red, caused by charged particles from the Sun passing along the Earth's magnetic field-lines and ionizing atmospheric gases as they converge near the Pole.

Ballistic
Propelled by the force of gravity. A **ballistic missile** is a projectile driven initially by the upward thrust of, eg., rocket power, then following its own trajectory. A **ballistic launch vehicle** is a launch vehicle (q.v.) without wings.

Booster
Lower stage of a launch vehicle (q.v.). The **boost phase** is the part of the trajectory from Earth to orbit powered by the booster.

Boost glider see **Sub-orbital airliner**

Burn-out
The point when a rocket engine stops functioning because it has used up all the fuel.

Centrifugal force
The force needed to make a body follow a circular path, eg the tension in the string when whirling a sling shot around your head, or the force of gravity keeping a satellite in orbit.

Design case
A set of conditions for which the strength and/or stiffness of an aeroplane structure is designed (and tested) to be adequate for the purpose for which it is to be used (eg. carrying passengers).

Drag
Resistance to an object's motion through the air.

Dynamic pressure
The air pressure on a body due to its motion. Dynamic pressure is proportional to the air density and, roughly, to the speed squared.

Flight envelope
Limitations of speed and height at which a vehicle is permitted to fly. The limitations may be due to strength, stiffness, stability or control.

Flyback booster
A booster fitted with wings, a tail and landing-gear so that it can be flown back to base after separation of the upper stages, either piloted or under radio control. It can then be refuelled and used again.

Fuel
The propellant of a liquid-fuelled rocket motor usually consists of a fuel and an oxidant stored in separate tanks. They burn together in the combustion chamber. The term is sometimes used to include both the fuel and the oxidant.

Fuel fraction
The ratio of weight of fuel carried to the total weight of a vehicle (ie. empty weight plus fuel weight plus payload).

Heavy lift vehicles
Large launch vehicles used to place big satellites in orbit. The Space Shuttle is the largest present-day Western launch vehicle, and is capable of carrying small hotel modules to orbit.

Hypersonic
At least five times faster than the speed of sound.

Jet engine
An engine in which fuel is burned together with oxygen from the air. See also **Ramjet**; **Turbo-jet**.

Knot
A measure of the speed of ships and aircraft: 1 UK knot = 6080 feet per hour or 1.853 kilometres per hour.

Launch vehicle
A vehicle designed to take off from Earth and carry a payload to orbit.

LH_2
Liquid hydrogen (see **Propellant**).

Lifecraft
The spaceliner's equivalent of lifeboats; used to evacuate passengers and crew to other hotels or back to Earth.

Liquid propellants
The liquid fuels and oxidants, such as liquid hydrogen and liquid oxygen, used to propel rocket-powered vehicles.

LOX
Liquid OXygen (see **Propellant**).

Mach number
A measurement of speed: the ratio of airspeed to the local speed of sound. Mach 1 equals the speed of sound (see also page 77).

Orbital velocity see **Satellite speed.**

Orbiter
The upper stage of a piloted launch vehicle, which carries the payload of passengers and/or cargo into orbit.

Payload
People and/or cargo carried by a vehicle.

Propellant
The chemicals used in rocket propulsion. They consist of a fuel (such as a liquid hydrogen or kerosene) and an oxidant, such as liquid oxygen. See also **Fuel**.

Ramjet
A jet engine (q.v.) consisting simply of a carefully-shaped pipe and a fuel injector. This is the simplest aircraft propulsion system, but it does not work below about Mach 1.5. A **turbo-ramjet** is a combined turbo-jet/ramjet.

Required structure mass
The mass left over for structure after the payload and fuel are accounted for.

Satellite
A man-made device sent into orbit around the Earth or other planets. A **commercial satellite** is paid for by the private sector, for profit, by contrast with government-funded satellites for research, defence or national prestige. A **communications satellite** is a relay station for telecommunications.

Satellite speed
The speed needed to remain in orbit around the Earth just above the atmosphere: about 17,500 mph or 28,000 kph. Also called **orbital velocity**.

Ski-jump
An inclined ramp fitted to the bow of the light aircraft carriers of the Royal Navy. Harrier fighters are catapulted along the deck and pushed up into the air by the ramp, giving the engines crucial extra seconds in which to accelerate the aeroplane to flying speed.

Solar radiation
The rays from the sun; more harmful in space as there is no atmosphere to act as a filter.

Solid propellants
The solid fuels and oxidants used to propel rocket-powered vehicles, such as the slow-burning gunpowder used in early rockets.

Spacebus
The authors' design for a second-generation spaceliner (q.v.) to follow Spacecab (q.v.)

Spacecab
The authors' design for a small spaceplane intended for minimum development cost.

Spacecraft
Any vehicle that travels in space. A satellite (q.v.), the Space Shuttle, a space hotel (q.v.) and a space station (q.v.) are all spacecraft.

Space debris
Particles, other than heavenly bodies, drifting in space. Space debris often results from the failure of man-made satellites or rockets.

Space hotel
A space station (q.v.) that can accommodate fare-paying tourists.

Space launcher see Launch vehicle.

Spaceliner
A spaceplane designed to carry passengers.

Spaceplane
A launch vehicle (q.v.) or spacecraft (q.v.) with wings, capable of taking off horizontally and flying into space. Like a launch vehicle, a spaceplane can carry smaller spacecraft into orbit.

Space station
A manned satellite.

Space tourism
Recreational space travel for the public.

SSTO
Single stage to orbit. A vehicle which reaches orbit without the use of staging (q.v.).

Staging
Mounting a series of vehicles on top of each other in order to achieve sufficient speed to launch satellites. Each state accelerates itself and the stages on top of it until it runs out of fuel, enabling the upper stages to reach orbit.

Structure weight fraction
The ratio of structure weight to total weight of a vehicle or stage (q.v.).

Sub-orbital airliner
An intercontinental airliner which accelerates to just short of satellite speed on the fringes of the atmosphere and then glides to its destination. Also called a **boost-glider**.

Subsonic
Slower than the speed of sound.

Supersonic
Faster than the speed of sound (Mach 1 see **Mach number**).

Thermal Protection
A layer of insulation to protect the structure of a spacecraft from the heat of re-entry. See also **Aerodynamic heating**.

Trajectory
The path a vehicle follows through the air or through space.

Turbo-jet
A jet engine (q.v.) in which all the air taken in passes through the combustion chamber, and which has a turbine and a compressor. See also **Ramjet**.

Wing-loading
The weight of a vehicle divided by wing area. Sailplanes have a low wing-loading; jet fighters a high wing-loading.

Zoom climb
The flight path of an aeroplane or a spaceplane which pulls up into a steep climb and then switches off its engines. From about Mach 4 it is possible to zoom climb to the fringe of space.

FURTHER READING

General

Cooper, Henry S.F. *A House in Space* Angus & Robertson 1977.

Francis, Peter and Jones, Pat *Images of Earth* Prentice-Hall 1984

Kelly, Kevin W. *The Home Planet* Queen Anne Press 1988

Koelle, D. and Kuczera, H. 'Sänger II, an advanced launcher system for Europe' *Acta Astronautica* 1989 Vol. 19, No. 1, pages 63-72

Rogers, T.F. 'Space settlements: Sooner than we think?' *Ad Astra* 1989 Vol. 1, No. 1, pages 30-34

White, Frank *The Overview Effect* Houghton Mifflin 1987

Woodcock, Gordon R. 'On the Economics of Space Utilisation' *Raumfahrtforschung*, Heft 3/1973

Yamanaka, T. and Nagatomo, M. 'Spaceports and new industrialized areas in the Pacific basin' *Space Policy* 1986 Vol. 2, No. 4, pages 342-354

Selected works by the authors

Ashford, D.M. 'Boost-Glide Vehicles for Long Range Transport' *Journal of the Royal Aeronautical Society* July 1965

Ashford, D.M. 'Space Tourism – Key to the Universe?' *Spaceflight* May 1984.

Ashford, D.M. and Collins P. Q. 'The Prospects for European Aerospace Transporters' Parts 1-4, *The Aeronautical Journal of the Royal Aeronautical Society* Vol. 93, Nos. 921-923, January, February and March, 1989. **Note: this paper forms the basis for the technical content of this book.**

Collins, P.Q. and Ashford, D.M. 'Potential Economic Implications of the Development of Space Tourism' *Acta Astronautica* Vol. 17, No. 4, 1988 pages 421-431

Collins, P.Q. and Ashford, D.M. An alternative to Hermes: A solution for the European space industry' *Space Policy*, 1988 Vol. 4, No. 4, pages 285-289

Collins, P.Q. 'European launch vehicle development: a commercial approach' *European Business Journal* 1989, Vol. 1, No. 2, pages 23-28

Collins, P.Q. 'Stages in the development of low Earth orbit tourism' *Space Technology* 1989 Vol. 9, No. 3, pages 315-23

Collins, P. Q. 'Space tourism – the door into the space age' *Analog Essays on Science* ed. S. Schmidt, pages 193-204 Wiley, 1990

ACKNOWLEDGEMENTS

Eddison Sadd Editions acknowledge with grateful thanks the contributions from the following people: Anthony Duke for paste-up and illustrations on pages 17, 30/31, 33, 35, 36, 37 (top), 40/41, 42/43, 50/51, 65, 71, 76/77, 102/103, 107, 108/109; Liz Eddison for illustration research; Sebastian Quigley (Linden Artists) for illustrations on the front and back of jacket and on pages 12/13, 23, 25, 26/27, 28/29, 37, 46/47, 51 BR, 53, 57, 58/59, 72/73, 74/75, 78/79, 80/81, 82/83, 86/87, 88/89, 113.

While every care has been taken to trace copyright owners the publishers would like to apologize to anyone whose copyright has been unwittingly infringed.

PICTURE CREDITS

T = top; B = bottom; C = centre; L = left; R = right

Aerospatiale pp32,106 C; Arianespace p44; Aviation Picture Library pp8, 10; British Aerospace pp62,106, 108; Fred Espenak/Science Photo Library: endpapers; Dr William C. Keel/Science Photo Library p100 BL; MBB p106; NASA pp63 TL, 63 TR, 65 T, 68, 92 T; NASA/Science Photo Library Front Cover (Background), pp1/2, 15, 18, 52 T, 52 B, 60, 63 B, 67, 85 T, 85 B, 91, 92 BL, 92 BR, 93 T, 93 B, 95 T, 95 B, 96 TL, 96 BL, 96/97 C, 97 TR, 97 BR, 98/99 C, 99 R, 104; Novosti p55; Ronald Royer/ Science Photo Library pp100 T, 101; John Sandford/ Science Photo Library p98 L; Science Photo Library pp77, 78, 94, 100 BR